Golf to
remember

By the same author:

Sudan Today
Kampala, City of the Seven Hills
The Great Opens

Golf to remember

Michael Hobbs
with
Peter Alliss

B.T. Batsford Ltd   London

For Matthew and Rachel

© Michael Hobbs 1978

First published 1978

ISBN 0 7134 1062 0

Filmset in Monophoto Apollo by
Servis Filmsetting Ltd, Manchester
Printed in Great Britain by
Redwood-Burn Ltd, Trowbridge & Esher
for the publishers B.T. Batsford Limited
4 Fitzhardinge Street, London W1H 0AH

Contents

Acknowledgment

My thanks are due to the following, who kindly supplied copyright photographs for the book: Peter Dazeley of Peter Dazeley Photography for the front jacket illustration, the jacket photograph of Peter Alliss, the colour photographs, and monochrome photographs 4, 5, 8–10, 19, 28, 30, 34; H.W. Neale of Action Photos for monochrome photographs 1–3, 6, 7, 11, 18, 20–27, 29, 31–33, 35–37; British Transport Hotels Ltd for monochrome photographs 12 and 13; Central Press Photos Ltd for monochrome photograph 17; Sport and General Press Agency for monochrome photographs 15 and 16; and The Times Picture Library for monochrome photograph 14.

The Illustrations

Introduction

When Peter and I first discussed the idea of this book one stark November day at Moor Allerton in Yorkshire, we began from the thought that no one had attempted a book on great rounds of golf. But it was an idea that had to be abandoned.

Why? Well eyewitness accounts of past feats are strangely lacking. What exist tend to be descriptions by the player himself of what he did and how he did it. This raised an immediate problem: all golfers are extremely boastful and they lie a lot – or at least omit the full story. You read, 'I hit an 8 iron to six feet and sank the putt', rather than, 'I thinned an 8 iron but thank God it caught the upslope and stopped quickly. Then I struck the putt far too hard but it hit the back of the hole, bounced up in the air and, glory be, fell in.'

Where then were the reporters of the day? Almost invariably they were in the wrong place. Lack of communications played a big part here; you just could not follow more than two or three games. X was favoured to win and all were watching him until by about the 14th it had become certain that he was going to have a very hard time indeed to break 80. Meanwhile, Mr Y was back in the clubhouse, card safely signed for a 68, and very much the centre of attention. But on the course he may well have had a following of three middle-aged ladies, two schoolboys who happened to come upon him while looking for birds' eggs, and a lame terrier.

So, as the day moved towards evening, we decided that to analyse great *achievements* in golf, rather than great rounds, would be a far more fruitful project on which to collaborate. This book is the result.

I must take responsibility for the writing and research. At the planning stage and throughout the writing of the book, Peter has read each section, commenting, criticizing and adding facts, experiences and anecdotes. We hope that our combined reminiscences and informed comment will serve as a worthwhile memorial to the great golfing achievements of the past.

MICHAEL HOBBS
Gateshead
October 1977.

Tournaments

Four major championships take place every year: the US Masters and PGA, and the British and US Opens. Then there are a host of tournaments of lesser status collectively worth the ransoms of many kings in the United States, Britain, Western Europe, Africa, Asia, Australasia . . . and still the list is by no means complete. It is a list that will expand again and again as the years pass, for golf is advancing from nation to nation at a pace and intensity unrivalled by any other sport.

As golf spreads, so does competitive golf. Yesterday, there were no golf courses in Morocco, Malawi, Russia, Thailand. Today there are and those that still have no open championship will tomorrow. In future years, some of these yet unborn championships will live on in the memory, while most will be as quickly forgotten as the details of what happened in the 1975 US Open. Though that one is so short a time ago, do *you* remember the name of the runner-up who led the field with one round to go or, even, who actually won it?

The chapter that follows is a selection of just a few of the championships and tournaments that have, to some extent, remained in the public memory and not always for the right reasons . . .

The best tournament of them all?

There are many candidates. What, for instance, about the 1972 British Open, which contained both Jack Nicklaus's splendid final round and, even more dramatic, the long-fought confrontation between the homeland hero, Tony Jacklin, and the Mexican desperado Lee Trevino, who holed long putts, chips and bunker shots on the bounce from all over the place? Or Bobby Jones playing that superb long iron from sand to defeat Al Watrous many years before? Or Palmer and Miller coming from well behind to win in the 1960 and 1973 US Opens? Or the 1977 gun-fight between Nicklaus and Watson at Turnberry . . . but my choice is the 1975 US Masters.

Central was the battle between Johnny Miller and Jack Nicklaus. For years no one had doubted that Jack Nicklaus was the best golfer in the world. He did not always win by any means but came to every competition as the bookmakers' favourite, the player all the others hoped would not be entered.

In the early months of 1975, this changed. It was no longer quite so obviously clear that Jack Nicklaus was the best of the best. *Perhaps* Johnny Miller was. In the early tournaments on the US circuit he had confirmed his unparalleled achievement in the 1973 US Open, when he shot a final-round 63, by setting a blistering pace that none could match. As he said, 'Happiness is knowing that even your poor shots are still quite good'. In golf history, only the young Horton Smith had so dominated the tour, more than three decades before.

So, there was talk of a match between Miller and Nicklaus, to establish who was the better of the two and make a lot of money for both promoter and protagonists.

Nicklaus would have none of it. He knows his golf history. In 1926 Walter Hagen had destroyed Bobby Jones in a match over 72 holes. The other side of the coin is that Hagen virtually never won a stroke-play competition if Jones was in the field. Two years later, Hagen himself was similarly put to rout by Archie Compston – and then won the British Open in a matter of days with Compston in the field. Any match or a stroke encounter proves only who was the best at a particular time and place. Nicklaus did not want the new image of being number two because of the publicity that would attend any loss to Miller.

But the battle between Miller and Nicklaus aside, there was another ingredient: the Third Man, Tom Weiskopf. He had been playing below the peaks since his 1973 victory in the British Open but in 1975 had returned to his best form. Many thought him the most talented striker of a golf ball in the game.

These then were the protagonists: Miller, Nicklaus and Weis-kopf. True, there were others who played very well indeed. Someone else, Bobby Nichols, led with 67 after the first round; another, Hale Irwin, recorded a course-record final 64, the lowest round of the Tournament. But although they came joint fourth, at no time did either seem at all likely to win the Masters.

Neither, after the first round, did Johnny Miller. He had been making much of the computer in his head that measured strength of wind, humidity, how much the greens were holding, and so on. He had a 75. Apparently the computer was working adequately but he consistently found himself between clubs for his second shots. Every one, he said, was either not quite a 4 iron and a few yards too long for a 5 iron, not quite a full wedge, not quite a 3 wood, a touch too long for a full 8 iron.

At that point Nicklaus was seven strokes ahead of him, after a 68, and one better than Tom Weiskopf. Nicklaus did better the next day with a 67. He had now built up a formidable lead on the whole field and was five shots clear of Arnold Palmer and Tom Watson, 11 ahead of Miller, who had 71, and six on Tom Weiskopf. Apart from Nicklaus, who had been putting inexorably, Weiskopf had played the best golf of the leaders but his second-round 72 had included sixes at the par-five 13th and 15th – both guarded by water but both birdie fours for drivers with Weiskopf's length. His ball had come to rest against a pine cone on one of them and at the other he had found an awkward lie.

So Nicklaus was in command, with an outside chance of beating his unapproached Masters record of 271, dating back ten years.

The drama began in the third round. Perhaps Nicklaus became cautious, tried to hold what he had. Weiskopf knew he had to go for everything. Miller might as well do the same; he was out of it anyway and had missed the cut only by three strokes. He could add to his reputation only by producing a couple of scintillating rounds, though they would, in all probability, still leave him in about sixth place.

Miller began with a par. He then birdied each of the following six holes (a record for the Augusta course as was his outward 30) and later added another at the 12th before parring his way home. This gave him a 65. Nicklaus had dropped strokes on the 1st, 9th, 11th and had had but two birdies to set against his errors. He had taken a one-over-par 73 and was now only three ahead of Miller, suddenly no longer out of it at all.

In fact Nicklaus no longer held the lead. Weiskopf had dropped a shot at the relatively easy 360-yard 3rd but had recorded seven birdies in his round. A 66 meant that he had gained seven shots on Nicklaus during the third day and now led the Tournament by a single shot.

It was all to play for again. Nicklaus, shaken by the evaporation of his lead, still knew he was the best player of a final round in the world. Perhaps. No one is likely to forget Miller's in the 1973 US Open. And ahead of them both, Tom Weiskopf.

Throughout, Nicklaus was playing about a hole ahead of Weiskopf and Miller, and was paired with Tom Watson. He began by dropping a shot on the 400-yard 1st hole, as a result of placing his tee shot into the woods. He then birdied three of the next four holes. Miller had similar results in the opening phase, dropping a shot on the 3rd but offsetting this handsomely with five birdies during the first nine holes. On a graph, Weiskopf would look the best: all pars or birdies to the turn. At this stage, Nicklaus had taken 35, Weiskopf 34 and Miller 32. With three and a half completed rounds Weiskopf looked the likely winner, for he lay two ahead of Nicklaus and Miller.

But tournaments no longer seem quite like that to either the leaders or the crowd on the course. What we and they are more aware of is the position against par for the number of holes each competitor has played. Let us look at it like that for the final holes of the 1975 Masters.

On the first four holes after the turn Nicklaus played par golf, Miller dropped and gained a shot, and Weiskopf dropped one. The 14th looked for a while as if it had settled the Tournament. Nicklaus deliberated long on his choice of club for the shot into the green on this 475-yard hole and certainly he had something absurdly lofted in his hands for a second shot to a hole of this length. Whatever the truth of it, he was short of the green, used a putter to come up the slope, was too bold, and his ball ran through the back. He had little chance of a four now and in fact had difficulty getting a five. Miller's troubles were more dramatic. He was in trees from the tee and hit another with his second shot. A bogey? A double bogey? Not a bit of it. Miller hit the flagstick with his third and then holed the three-feet putt. Weiskopf, on the other hand, had no trouble at all. He was two yards away in two shots and holed for a birdie. The scoreboards showed: Weiskopf − 11; Nicklaus − 10; Miller − 9.

The 15th at Augusta National is 520 yards long and therefore a par four for the likes of Nicklaus, Miller and Weiskopf – except for two things. The green is fronted by water and when you have cleared that it is still very easy to run through the back. What is needed is a huge drive so that a lofted shot can be played into the green; anything of low trajectory may well fly through the green and onwards, as Nicklaus had experienced in other Masters tournaments, when at least once he had reached water far behind the green.

Nicklaus hit a good drive but it still left him a long way to go. He wanted to take a 1-iron but was hitting into a light breeze; he felt a wood was necessary to give him sufficient length. He waited for the breeze to drop. Few noticed the delay; Nicklaus always ponders every shot. Eventually the breeze slacked and Nicklaus went quickly with a 1-iron. There was no pause while he followed the flight of the ball. Nicklaus knew it was good and marched after it like a man confident of glory. His ball was flying straight for the flag and amply long enough to clear the water. It pitched and stopped towards the rear of the green. He lagged his putt towards the hole and tapped in for a birdie. Nicklaus said later that it had been the finest 1-iron shot he had hit since 1967 (referring to one that had won him the US Open). The carry had been about 230 yards, while the flag had been about 245 yards from Nicklaus.

Weiskopf followed him a few minutes later with a 4-iron which ran through the green; Miller played a 3 wood that settled down on the green but well to the right. Weiskopf chipped boldly – too boldly – and was four yards past. He marked his ball and waited for Miller to try his 12-yard putt. Miller coasted just past the hole but had his birdie four. As Weiskopf putted he knew he had to hole it not to lose the Tournament. It went straight into the middle. Weiskopf − 12; Nicklaus − 11; Miller − 10.

The 16th is where Henry Longhurst describes the downfall of the mighty in rotund tones for the TV audience. The hole measures 190 yards and all of that, except for the last few feet, is over water with more water to the left. There are bunkers behind the green to dissuade anyone from playing 'safe' and taking a bigger club to be sure of clearing the water. Regulars come to watch year after year, sometimes choosing their spot and staying there for hours before the first competitor is due.

Nicklaus hit his tee shot a little heavily and regarded the flight of his ball with distaste. 'Get up,' he called out. It cleared the water but pitched well short of the flag and then rolled back down the slope until it was about 14 yards away from the hole. The scene now switches to his playing partner, Tom Watson, still in with a remote chance of winning. Alas poor Tom. He needed two balls in the water before he managed to persuade one onto the green. That was a seven for him and goodbye till next year. Better days at Carnoustie lay ahead.

Nicklaus looked his putt over anxiously. If he was short, his ball would run back down the slope and finish not far from his feet. If he was long, he would be left with a downhill putt back – and that one could just possibly carry on past the hole, and on and on.

Nicklaus conceals his emotions well, though of recent years he has learned to smile and wave to his gallery (he has also found that it is better public relations to be slim rather than fat, and has cultivated medium-length hair rather than a crewcut). But when that huge putt dropped into the hole he leapt and ran across the green. Miller later said, 'I have never seen Jack jump around like that. I was happy to walk through the Bear prints.'

Weiskopf, who had just saved himself the Tournament with his four-yard putt, was watching from the tee. He now had to par the hole to stay level with Jack Nicklaus. And the 16th had done him no good at all the previous year when he had found the water and thus lost to Player.

Like Nicklaus's, his iron shot was heavy and only just cleared the water. He was about 40 yards from the hole though on the green. Miller came in pin high, but about 35 feet away. Weiskopf's first putt was quite good and looked as if it just might reach the hole but it did not quite make it, tailed away, and ran back and to the left. He now had a curving, uphill 18-feet putt left. Miller putted up close and tapped in; Weiskopf missed narrowly. On the course, Nicklaus stood -12; Weiskopf -11; Miller -10.

Two par fours remained, the 400-yard 17th and the 420-yard

18th. All three drove well at the next and played approach shots with 8 irons of nearly equal quality. Nicklaus was about 15 feet away and putted like a man who does not want to give anything away to the opposition. His putt never looked like going in but always looked dead. He tapped in for par.

Weiskopf's approach had run to the back of the green and he too putted the four yards cautiously, perhaps now a man with thoughts of holding second place. Nevertheless, his ball finished only a foot away and he holed that one. Miller's putt was easily the shortest of the three and he watched it curl up, across the slope – and in.

Nicklaus, about to putt on the last hole, stopped at the roar from the gallery and waited for the scoreboard to show who had holed. If Miller had, this would leave him still one behind; if Weiskopf, they would be joint leaders at − 12.

When he saw that it was Miller, he bent down again to his putt of about eight feet. Again he prodded it cautiously and the ball stopped short but left him with a safe par, a final-round of 68, and a total of 276. He was content to wait it out and see if either Miller or Weiskopf could birdie the last and earn a playoff.

Miller drove safely and Weiskopf followed with the longest drive of the Tournament at the 18th hole, about 30 yards further than anyone else had driven. Miller's approach then came in to the right-hand half of the green, a little past the hole. He would have a downhill putt of about 15 feet with a right to left borrow on it. Weiskopf's shorter approach (he needed just a 9 iron) was then punched in and it bit and spun back. He had much the same line to the hole as Johnny Miller but about half the distance to go.

If Miller had been able to watch TV a few minutes before he would have seen Tom Watson hole almost exactly the same putt for a face-saving birdie (remember Tom's seven at the 16th?). But Miller's putt always looked as if it had been struck too directly at the hole. The borrow took it past the lower edge by about two inches.

Had Weiskopf learnt anything? He consulted his caddy, who told him to go for the right lip of the hole. Weiskopf struck it firmly, perhaps a little too strongly. It made for a point an inch or so to the right – and kept on going.

So Nicklaus, for the fifth time, put on the green jacket traditionally presented by the previous year's winner to the new champion. For Weiskopf, it was that second place, jointly with Miller, that no one is supposed to remember. But we all remember how Roberto de Vicenzo lost the Masters because of signing an incorrect scorecard in 1968, while not so many remember the winner, Bob Goalby. Perhaps the 1975 Masters will live on in memory not only by the name of its winner but because of the three men who made it, in the words of Jack Nicklaus, 'The most exciting day of golf I can remember in 15 years'.

How they finished:

276	Nicklaus	68, 67, 73, 68
277	Miller	75, 71, 65, 66
	Weiskopf	69, 72, 66, 70
282	Hale Irwin and Bobby Nichols.	

Worse be . . .

Few indeed have been the golfers who have won love from followers of the game. Respect, yes, for such as Ben Hogan, whom nearly everyone called 'Mr' and might have been chilled by an icy glare had they ventured to say 'Ben'. Or Jack Nicklaus, who has little time for fools or foolish questions but all the time in the world for anyone who can spark his thoughts about the game of golf. But from such as these the wary keep their distance. If wise, you go and watch them, keep your mouth shut and speak only when spoken to. There may then be rewards. A friend of mine, for example, a few years ago decided to follow Bob Charles rather early one morning in a run-of-the-mill tournament. Bob appears to be the most taciturn of them all, but that morning as he shanked one there and topped another there, en route to a score somewhere in the not-so-low 80s, he chatted amiably and profanely.

Golf, in fact, brings out the best in not very many of us. We chat gaily only when we are playing really rather well and ought to notice that no one is being charmed by us: they are far too consumed with irritation by the horrors of their own game on that particular day and wish we would be quiet.

Again, the game induces introspection. The player is constantly reflecting on the position of the hands on the shaft, what he might be doing that he ought not with his left hip, weight transference, whether or not the hands and wrists are just so at the top of the backswing, why he cannot stop coming across the ball at impact, and so on and so on.

Pity then the golfer who, whatever the level of his accomplishment, is for 99.99 per cent of his minutes on a golf course acutely disturbed by his continued failure to be able to perform a simple sequence of movements with moderate efficiency. Yet there have been a few who have been able to rise above such constant soul searching and have been loved for the man that exists quite separately from the golfer: Bobby Jones, for instance, who, however often and intensely he found it necessary to grind and clench his teeth, was always the epitome of courtesy both on and off the course; and Roberto de Vicenzo.

Roberto came regularly to the British Open. Year after year he finished high up but after 20 years in the attempt he was obviously too old by 1967 when at last he pulled it off, quelling Gary Player and Jack Nicklaus, the holder, at Hoylake on the final day. Roberto is a born golfer but has never lost delight in practising. His ideal way to spend a day is to hit golf balls on the practice ground for a few hours and when all is going well he will finally go out and play a round. But the man was often a poor putter, claimed it was agony for him, but persisted in trying to find a method that would be at least moderately reliable – he had long given up the ambition to be a super putter. Eventually he did for a spell manage it.

One reward was the 1967 British Open, just about the most popular of golf victories. But remember that Roberto's relatively poor putting stroke made him a failure only as regards winning the major championships. After all, just a select few have won more than a hundred tournaments as Roberto has. Perhaps his putting was by no means as bad as all that.

The following year saw him at Augusta, Georgia, for the US Masters. In any major championship the drama is likely to be largely compressed into the final day and in 1968 this was especially so at Augusta. Player was again one of Roberto's main rivals for the title. When the last day began, this was the position:

In all there were 16 within four shots of Player, so in these circumstances Roberto did not have a vast following when he set out with Tommy Aaron for the last round.

For the 1st hole you drive over a ravine which does not usually give a class player any cause for fear and then, if you can hit the majestic, long, drawn shots of a Vicenzo, you would expect to have just an 8 or 9 iron left for the shot to the green at this 400-yard hole. Roberto struck a 9 iron, the ball came in nicely over a greenside bunker, pitched a few yards short of the hole and shortly afterwards rolled in. Eagle! With that shot Roberto had almost overtaken Gary Player, who was out last. The next is a par five of some 550 yards. He got his 'regulation' birdie, and at the 360-yard 3rd hole very nearly holed his approach shot once more. Never mind, it is always refreshing to have a putt of just a foot for a birdie. Roberto was suddenly four under par for the first three holes and led the Tournament. Of course, this kind of stuff was what dreams are made of, and the dream did not continue. Instead, Roberto played steadily to the turn. He birdied the 8th and had pars on the rest.

At this point he stood at nine under par for the Tournament, while Devlin was eight under and Bob Goalby seven under. Roberto was bunkered at the next hole but came out to about a yard and safely got the putt in. At the next he drilled a 4 iron along the edge of the pond onto the green to about three yards and two-putted for par. Rae's Creek is the main feature on the 12th, a 155-yard par three. Roberto hit a 6 iron safely over it and holed a putt of some four yards for a birdie. At this point Roberto was looking the winner, with the main threat coming from Bob Goalby.

Goalby, like Roberto, is also a right-to-left player but whereas the Argentinian struck the ball with draw, Bob was always fighting a disastrous hook. But that day the fight was going well. In their play of the 13th the fight went even better for Goalby. He got a birdie, whereas Roberto was bunkered near the green with his second, blasted on and needed two putts. So the gap was but a single shot. Bob had not exactly played the hole more adeptly, but it does no harm at all to get a putt in from off the green. On the 15th, that dramatic hole where the long second is played over water and when that has been cleared there is always the possibility of the ball running through the green and on, and on, into more water, Roberto pitched his third shot to about three yards and holed the putt. Bob Goalby did better. He sent in a 3 iron and then holed out for an eagle three.

But it was the final two holes that provided the most drama of all. On the 17th, a par four of about 400 yards, Roberto, playing two holes ahead of Goalby, needed just a pitching wedge for his second shot into the green and it was a beauty. Birdie. Goalby was less efficient. He three-putted. That was a five to him as opposed to Roberto's three.

But Roberto's marker, Tommy Aaron, did not write down the number '3'. Absentmindedly, no doubt thinking of the shots of his own that had not gone any too well, he wrote '4'. However, it hardly mattered. Roberto at the end of the round had only to query it; Tommy would have said something like, 'Oh hell! Yes. Wedged it to a yard or so, didn't you, and made the putt.' He would no doubt have then changed that number from a '4' to a '3' and initialled the correction. And if Tommy did not in fact remember clearly (hardly likely after the passage of just ten minutes or so) there were the thousands on the course who had seen it all and multi-millions following the closing stages on TV.

And so Roberto came to the last and hit a fair enough drive which erred on the side of caution – a careful one rather than a full-out flash of the club. He had a longish iron to the green rather than the shortish pitch he might have liked but this should have been a minor problem, for Roberto was striking the ball superbly. He used a 4-iron and pulled the shot somewhat. His ball came to rest at the foot of a bank a little to the left of the green. He chipped it to about three yards and missed the putt. Ruefully he made his way from the final green, his mind occupied only with thoughts of how he really most definitely should not have pulled that 4-iron shot and then the chip had not been struck quite cleanly.

He looked at the card, his eyes perhaps seeing only that five on the last that should have been a four. Never mind a 65 was, and still is, just one shot above the Augusta course record.

A little later Goalby came to the last also having just three-putted the 17th. Fighting his likely hook he sliced it into the trees but many yards from the hole. Bob got down in two and there would have to be a playoff between them the next day.

But there was not. A player is responsible for checking his score on each hole, though not for the total. Roberto knew he had a 65 and signed for it, yet the four that Aaron had written down for the 17th passed unnoticed. It made his total 66 and that meant Goalby was the outright winner by a single shot. Unless there was a way round.

Bobby Jones was brought into it as the founder of the Tournament back in 1934, and he would dearly have liked to have found that way round if this could have been done without bending the Rules of Golf. He was told that bending, if not indeed breaking, would undoubtedly be necessary and Jones made it clear that Roberto's four would have to stay.

Goalby was the winner. Poor Bob. If there had been a playoff it is as likely as not that he would have won it. Instead, he found himself a winner that no one, except the record books, remembers, while Roberto is remembered as the man who *really* won and was disqualified which, of course, he was not. The four he had signed for had to stand; only his three was disqualified.

Said Roberto, 'What a stupid I am to be wrong in this wonderful Tournament'. That remark did him no harm at all, and did indeed win him a trophy of another kind, the William D. Richardson award for sportsmanship. Roberto is a delightful conversationalist but not a man for speeches. When he was called to his feet to accept the trophy he said a very few words only. They were to the effect that, well, here he was being honoured by the sports writers of America for having made a mistake about a number. And what little mistake had they made? The word-mongers had spelled his name wrongly on the menu, the seating list and the trophy itself! Short though it was, the speech went down very well.

Roberto's mistake undoubtedly brought him more fame, particularly in the US where he had never done as well as he might, than had his British Open win the year before. He later reckoned that his clerical error had brought him publicity worth at least a quarter of a million dollars. If he had spotted Tommy Aaron's mistake and had it corrected he would have made very little at all. For if Roberto and Bob Goalby had met in a playoff, even if Roberto had won, the drama would have been at a routine level.

Most of us tend to think that if we should happen to win the US Open or Masters or the British Open we should overnight become millionaires. But it does not work out quite as simply as this. A British winner of the British Open could expect this result as could an American winner of the US Open. Winners of the Masters do well (quite apart, of course, from the very substantial prize money) only if they are golfers in the top half dozen or so. Thus Tony Jacklin, for instance, made a fortune from his 1969 British Open and very little directly from his 1970 US win. On balance, if you want to make a quick fortune, aim for the British Open because a host of contracts in South Africa, Australia, New Zealand, Japan and the remainder of the English-speaking world will tend to fall into your eager lap. But you would still need someone with the negotiating power of a Mark McCormack to manage you.

But championship golf is, in the end, about more than money. Roberto, despite his grace and charm at the time, was forcing the wry smiles and the jokey remarks. For a while he lost interest in golf and in the lonely but delightful hours of practice. Eventually he was to add a remark to sum up the whole affair that I think deserves to survive a while longer: 'Worse be if you go across the street and you no see the car.'

'Only'

Carnoustie does not change much. In 1968 it was described as the toughest course that had ever been presented to a British Open field and much the same kind of thing was said about it in 1975. In that year, the course Hale Irwin called a 'sleeping giant' did indeed sleep through the first three days of the Championship. On the final day there was no more than a stiff breeze, but few indeed matched par.

In 1937 the weather was less kind and greatness was required to win. Gathered there were the best of the day. There had been a

Ryder Cup match and the US team had stayed on to compete. They had won for the first time in Britain but the British Open title had been in British hands since Densmore Shute's victory at St Andrews in 1933.

There were qualifying rounds which seemed to show that the reason British professionals – Cotton, Perry and Padgham – had been carrying it off was that fewer Americans had been competing. But now there was weight of numbers from over the Atlantic, the ten members of the US Ryder Cup team and their non-playing captain, Walter Hagen. British opinion in the Press and the street was that no one could beat them. Bernard Darwin reflected the current despair by writing of 'these swarms of Americans who do 72s like clockwork'. He beheld the young Sam Snead who 'played an iron shot of a quality to bring tears to the eyes' and felt no one could look more a champion. Yet Henry Cotton, before hostilities began, had felt that four 75s would be good enough to win it and that a couple of 80s might do well enough if the winds blew on the last day, when 36 holes would be played.

Horton Smith made nonsense of that over the two qualifying rounds. He had a pair of 69s and led by three shots over such other Americans as Gene Sarazen on 141 and then Sam Snead, Byron Nelson and Walter Hagen on 142. On 144 was the then slender figure of Bobby Locke, now beginning 20 years at the top. At last there was an Englishman. Cotton had managed to total 145.

Of course, those qualifying rounds, now long forgotten, never did *prove* anything, but they established a mood and the phalanx of Americans at the top must have seemed a group of warriors that would inevitably be there at the end of the day. Bernard Darwin felt that they would not all 'fall down dead at once'. Nor did they.

But when the Championship proper began they by no means reeled off their 72s. The course had been stretched to its full length and the wind was from east instead of west. The 7,200 yards took a toll. Of course an American, Ed Dudley, led by two clear shots at the end of the day but, surprise, three British held second place with 72s – W.J. Branch, R.A. Whitcombe (the most talented but perhaps the most erratic of the Whitcombe brothers) and Alf Padgham.

Padgham the previous year had dominated the British circuit as no one before or since has done. He had made all of golf seem as simple as, in theory, it is. The drives had gone down the middle and the iron shots had rifled at the flag. Thereafter he had stood rather a long way from the ball and swung the putts into the hole.

Peter Alliss recalls how Alf became an exceptional putter instead of merely a moderate one. Padgham had always found it easy to play his chips up to the hole from the edge of the green with a 5- or 6-iron, but was far less assured in then getting the thing into the hole. Logically enough, he decided to employ his chipping technique to the putting stroke and in due course appeared on the circuits with a blade putter that was a few inches longer than the implements he used customarily for chipping and, of course, a good deal straighter in the face. Peter remembers it as being ideally balanced and having a shaft that was sheathed in some yellow material. The implement chosen, Alf settled into his normal feet-spread-wide stance, stood well back from the ball (most unusual this) and chipped the ball into the hole.

But in 1937 the game had ceased to be at all easy for Alfred Padgham. His 72 in this first round at Carnoustie was a welcomed surprise, for Alf had been making golf look very difficult indeed throughout the year. But perhaps the obvious simplicity of the thing was now coming back to him again?

Horton Smith, of the first 'mechanical swing', product of steel shafts, and silky putting touch, was already looking less of a sure-fire favourite: he had taken 77, not an ultimate disaster, but equally not the form of his pair of 69s in the qualifying rounds. All in all, perhaps the home players did have a chance for, instead of the expected mass of Americans poised at the top, there was only Ed Dudley, leading on 70, then three British, followed by the methodical, seemingly rock-steady Shute on 73 and then a bunch of British players.

The second day belonged to the Whitcombe brothers. R.A. had added a 70 – equal best round of the Championship proper – to his 72. Brother Charles lay but two shots behind, together with Ed Dudley who had taken four shots more for his second round. But the American challenge was no longer as inevitable as it had seemed. Only one more of them, Shute, lay within five shots of the leader. However, stretch it to six, and you then had Horton Smith and Walter Hagen. A shot further away were Ralph Guldahl (twice to win the US Open) and Sam Snead. Two shots more back were Byron Nelson and Charles Lacey. Today, Nelson would be thought well out of it. But in 1937, every champion was felt likely to play one rather poor round in the high 70s. Nelson had recorded his mid-70 rounds. A couple of 71s, or the like, would still see him home.

'Thank God,' said the British, 'Henry isn't leading.' Henry Cotton was lying very handily, thank you very much, on 146. The British preferred him to be a little off the lead. Three years before, they had endured Royal St George's, where he had entered the final round with a nine-stroke lead and had then seemingly attempted to throw it all away. True, he had won comfortably in the end but the consensus was that Henry was not comfortable if a tournament were almost in his pocket. There was the reputation for 'temperament' (whatever that is) and the collapse in the final round. As regards the Open Championship, this was more or less true of Cotton's scoring in the late 1920s and early 1930s. He *did* seem to have the habit of manoeuvring himself into a useful position on the first two days and then drifting away on the final day (remember that the Open was, until relatively recently, played with a couple of rounds on the last day).

Many years later Ken Venturi won immortality by perceptibly staggering his way through the last two rounds of a US Open and having a doctor insisting on accompanying him around the course after lunch. 'Heat exhaustion', they called it, but Venturi won. Great heat is indeed something that most golfers dislike; poor golfers almost invariably dislike playing in a stiff breeze, let alone a gale: that not-too-well hit, cutty little drive will become a curling right angle of a slice. The best strikers in the field rejoice. The outcome of the contest will not this time depend quite so much on the chipping and putting. If the strike at the flag is true, the ball with bore through the wind – no matter really if you have to hit a 4 iron instead of a pitching wedge.

But rain is everybody's enemy and that final day at Carnoustie it rained continuously, always heavily, sometimes a deluge. The golfer who fails to keep his grips dry (always leather at that time) is as lost as a musketeer with damp powder or those French crossbowmen who fought at Agincourt with wet bow strings.

By the end of the third round Reginald Whitcombe still led by the same two strokes, followed by his brother Charles. Cotton was one stroke further off, confidence increasing. The 453-yard last hole had done him no harm at all. He had hit a vast drive, a relaxed-looking iron and then down went the putt. In the circumstances his 73 was a very good round indeed and those few that bettered it were clawing their way up the field from perhaps too far behind. One of them was Byron Nelson, later to become part of golfing legend by putting together the longest spell of low scoring ever likely to be done. He had a 71, which put him on 222 with Densmore Shute, still the most feared of the American invasion.

Throughout his round Cotton had driven well but his iron shots had often failed to hit and hold the greens. But from that point on, the hours upon hours of practice for which Cotton had become renowned seemed to have paid off. Again and again he had chipped precisely up to the hole and single-putted.

So it was out into the deluge again, after a light lunch. At the 401-yard 1st, Cotton missed the green but was down after a chip and a putt. At the next, another 400-yarder, he was safely on, some eight yards from the hole, and struck the putt right into the centre. At the next three holes he missed the green each time; but each time he contrived a par. At the 6th, the longest hole on the course, he was nearly on in two shots and the chip-and-a-putt habit remained. That was two under par, figures that only one other player in contention matched.

The Whitcombe brothers meanwhile kept going. Nevertheless, both drifted a little and finished with 76s. For Reg, this might still have been good enough and he achieved it despite the fact that on one tee shot his driver flew from his hands and the ball went nowhere.

At the 7th Cotton dropped a shot, but still he turned in 35. He must by then have known that he ought to be the winner if he could keep it going. At the short 13th he missed the green but chipped dead. Much the same thing happened at the next but at the 15th he at last missed a short putt. By now Cotton's task was clear cut. He had to finish 4, 4, 5 to win on holes for which the par any day is $3\frac{1}{2}$, $4\frac{1}{2}$, $4\frac{1}{2}$. The 16th at Carnoustie, then and today, offers a simple problem: if you can hit a straight shot about 230 yards with some bite on it then your ball has a fair chance of holding the crowned green – put another way, the 16th is one of the most difficult par threes in the world. Cotton got his three and faced the problems of the 17th. Here a golfer can attempt to carry the Barry Burn and will then be left with no more than a mid iron to the green. Few ever attempt this carry; none when an open championship is within their grasp. So, you play short of the burn with a long iron and have then to play another long iron, or a wood, to a distant green. The shot must either be flown directly at the flag, in which case it has to carry bunkers that lurk in waiting over a brow, or you can fade it in through a gap and hope that the bank on the left of the green is kind to you and brings the ball down towards the flag.

Cotton's second shot hit a spectator but he pitched well and then sank a good putt. Now he had 'only' to get a six to win. 'Only' is one of the most abused words in golfing vocabulary. I can remember not long ago winning a monthly medal myself with a – for me – distinctly blistering finish of 2, 4, 3 against a par of 3, 5, 4. But no one had been saying to me that I had 'only' to do anything at all, for I had been knocking the ball along in very moderate fashion. So there was no tension or thoughts of winning. Without concern, I happened to strike three successive pitches fairly precisely and the resultant putts would have required some care to miss them. But what of the man who finished second? Off something like a 16 handicap, he was playing the round of his life and on the 16th tee stood only two or three shots over par. 'Well, Jimmy,' they said, 'Don't top it into the bushes at this hole or hook too many out of bounds at the next and you're home. You've only got to keep on your feet.'

Well Jimmy got past the 16th without more than the odd shot or two dropped to par. The tee shot at the 17th normally presented no particular problem: on the left, a lateral water hazard; beyond that, a wall and the out of bounds. And Jimmy faded every wooden-club shot, though the unkind sometimes refer to the performance as a slice. There followed three successive prettily-struck hooks, all comfortably out of bounds, and he did not play the last hole too well either.

That is the trouble with that word 'only' in golf. It conjures up for golfers at each and every level thoughts of how impossible, absurd, stupid, and a whole variety of other adjectives, it would be *not* to win; worse still, if both glory and money are vamping you.

But Cotton did win. He hit a goodish tee shot and then said to himself, 'I mustn't hook this next one out of bounds to the left'. Instead he hit it very firmly indeed with a 2 iron into a greenside bunker on the right. Now he faced a handicap golfer's problem: if he took it too cleanly off the rain-packed sand, it might fly straight over the green and the fence out of bounds. Cotton took an 8 or 9 iron instead of a sand wedge (they do not perform too reliably from that kind of surface), punched it out onto the green and then followed with a couple of putts. That was a 71.

'Only' one other opponent remained, the rain. As Cotton played the last few holes, the sheeting rain had become a deluge. If the greens had become totally waterlogged the fourth round would have been cancelled and it would have been all to do again. Cotton waited, not to see if there was anyone who could catch him with a sudden sequence of superlative shots, but in the hope that the Carnoustie turf would prove sufficiently absorbent.

All was well, and this is what the papers printed after Henry Cotton had accepted the cup for a second time:

290	T.H. Cotton	74, 72, 73, 71
292	R.A. Whitcombe	72, 70, 76, 76
293	C. Lacey	76, 75, 70, 72
294	C.A. Whitcombe	73, 71, 74, 76
296	Byron Nelson	75, 76, 71, 74

Cotton, since the very early 1930s, had been accepted by most as the best British golfer, although he seemed unable to win the Open. His 1934 victory had removed that taint but opinions persisted that on that occasion there had been 'only' one or two Americans and this despite the fact that they included Gene Sarazen and Densmore Shute, who had won the Open the two previous years. Nevertheless, if the number of bodies is what really matters, in 1937 there was the whole US Ryder Cup team scattered behind Cotton.

But it ought to be remembered that a British linksland course sets problems of a kind that are different from those normally faced by Americans. The measure of American superiority was, and now even more emphatically is, that a Palmer, Hogan, Lema or Watson can arrive, have a brief look around and immediately (or, in the case of Palmer, after a second look) win the British Open.

One of the great 'might-have-beens' of British golf is that Cotton did not pit himself against America's best on their home grounds during his best years, from 1934 to the Second World War. If he had, and had also succeeded, he would have edged himself a step further up the ladder of golfing immortality.

He did play in the United States early in the 1930s, and formed a trio with Aubrey Boomer and Percy Alliss who, during this spell, tied with Walter Hagen in the 1931 Canadian Open. Cotton found that he needed to change his swing to compete with US length from the tee and his efforts to change from a fade to draw unsettled him. So too did boils! Later on, in 1948, he again played the US circuit but on this occasion it may be that his interest was more in building his physical fitness than in winning tournaments. This was in the aftermath of war when journalists were always writing that the reason British sportsmen could not win was that they were all half-starved due to food rationing. However, while Cotton was not doing great things in America, in the summer that followed he won the British Open at Muirfield for a third time.

Since his great days, only Jacklin amongst British players has at all comparably achieved similar greatness and of him one must use the word 'only'. The 'only' this time refers to time span: for a year Jacklin was, it could well be argued, the best golfer in the world. But is that so much to set against a Sam Snead who at the dawn of his career in 1937 went round Carnoustie in 75, 74, 75, 76 and 40 years on, though like Sinatra 'retired', would be expecting tomorrow to do a good bit better than that?

Cotton's Carnoustie victory set the final seal of public approval on his reputation. His name became synonymous with golf. He appeared, topping the bill, at the London Palladium and was much seen in his splendid Mercedes, when ownership of any vehicle was a rarity amongst British professional golfers. This in itself was merely outward evidence that Henry had 'made' it. In fact, by making it so emphatically Cotton helped to raise the status of golf professionals as a whole in Britain just as Walter Hagen had done ten years or so earlier for his American counterparts. More important though, Britain had now an international golfer of the highest class for the first time since the fading memories of Vardon, Taylor and Braid.

The second era

Jack Nicklaus's form, maintained now for approaching two decades, makes it impossible to say that anyone in golf history was emphatically greater than he. Yet there are a handful of candidates for Olympus whose case can be argued. Hogan, for instance, who played his most successful golf on legs damaged in a road accident that came very near to killing him. As we go further back in time, direct evidence becomes less available and we meet golfers that were different in kind because they played courses in far less manicured condition and swung implements that required a drastically different technique. Jones, for example, won all his championships using hickory shafts, a lively wood but one undeniably more difficult to control. The material does not let a golfer swing full out, for the clubhead tends to twist on the shaft, whereas a steel shaft only flexes forwards and backwards.

So far I have mentioned names that were the greatest of their eras – indeed created the era itself. We could, for example, call the 1960s and 1970s the age of Nicklaus, while the 1920s belong to Robert Tyre Jones. Such men, by their dominance, have defined both the ends and beginnings of phases of golf history – 1923 is one such beginning because it marked Jones's first Open victory while his Grand Slam of 1930 did not merely put the last full stop on a page, it killed off the era.

Two other distinct eras remain: Young Tom Morris's brief shooting star from 1868 to 1872 and the reign of the Great Triumvirate of Taylor, Vardon and Braid from the mid-1890s to the First World War. These thoughts appear to have knocked a few periods of golf history on the head – which comes close to proving my point. Interest in golf declined for several years after Jones's departure. The king is dead but long live . . . who?

So it was also after Young Tom Morris's early death. No successor appeared for more than 20 years when John Henry Taylor, first in time of the Great Triumvirate, won his first Open and repeated his success the following year. Many thought that he had set new standards of excellence and that an undisputed reign would continue. Taylor did not hit the gutta percha ball of the day an exceptional distance; what he did supremely well was to place the ball rather near the flag with every mid-iron shot, managing to work more backspin onto the ball than had before been achieved.

But a rival appeared able to achieve the same standard of result from a greater distance with a wood – Harry Vardon. His was also a distinctive style. Today we think of the high-flying shots of a Weiskopf, Nicklaus or Miller as typical, whereas the lower flight of a Trevino is cause for comment. But British golfers, at least until after the First World War, regarded wind as an almost constant element to be fought. The early Scottish golf courses were nearly all situated on seaside linksland and much the same held good for English courses. Therefore golfers developed techniques of striking aimed at keeping the ball low, under the wind. Vardon did not and those watching him for the first time wondered if his game would not be blown to pieces every time the winds blew.

Speculations of the same kind are voiced today when the players gather for a British Open. A Miller or Weiskopf's chances are thought to be lessened in anything other than a dead calm. Events have shown that this is not so, for what counts is not how high the flight but how well the ball is struck. A slightly-cut high shot into a left-to-right wind becomes a slice in short time but otherwise a straight hit rarely fails to hold its line. This being so, judgment – whether you play high or low shots – becomes the key factor, for a tailwind carries your ball further and reduces its backspin on landing, while a headwind of course has the opposite effect. The trick is to be able to judge precisely the degree of effect.

Vardon had such judgment in high degree and, of course, could vary the pattern of his shot as well as the next man. Although the easy swing seemed not to vary, at the moment of impact his huge hands would be hooding the clubface to get more run on the ball, kept more ahead than usual in a punchy shot fired in low at the flag, or perhaps cutting across so that the ball would float in from right to left.

Studying the line: Jack Nicklaus and Tony Jacklin

It's in! Lee Trevino and Gary Player

Seven British Open titles between them: Henry Cotton and Bobby Locke

Mildred 'Babe' Zaharias

Where's that one going? Gary Player, David Graham, Jack Nicklaus and Arnold Palmer

The King's Course, Gleneagles

The 8th green at Turnberry before the 1977 British Open

As the Open Championship of 1896 approached Taylor was the man to beat, but at Vardon's club, Ganton in Yorkshire, the members were not so sure. They put up the money for a match between the two before the Open. Over 36 holes Harry Vardon won by eight and seven.

In June it was time for Muirfield, a course disparaged by an expert of the day, Andrew Kirkaldy, as 'an old water meadie'. Perhaps it was then not quite the strictest and fairest test of golf that many think it today, but Kirkaldy's comment was probably prompted by the fact that the course was more lush than the other Scottish links this player was accustomed to. Harold Hilton had won the last time the Open had been held here in 1892 and he would be there again. As *The Times* of the day put it: 'It is gratifying that Mr Hilton has seen his way to come North for the meeting.' This comment suggests, I think, that the Open had yet to be seen as an event that every leading golfer always attended. It really was praiseworthy of Harold to venture so far north from his native Liverpool. Some of the other leading amateurs, such as the mighty John Ball, did not bother.

Nevertheless all the leading professionals were there, spurred on by the fortune to be won – £30 for the winner as well as a gold watch worth £10. Even second place was good for £20, but no gold watch, alas. Taylor was, of course, the favourite and he began with scoring that made it seem he might well walk away with the Championship: out in 35, even today very respectable scoring but outstanding with a gutta percha ball. He faltered on the return journey, however, and took 42 for a total of 77. Although there was no par there was a 'standard score of the green' and this was reckoned to be about 78. But all the talk at the end of the day was of Alex Herd, who had astounded all the other competitors by going round in 72. As *The Times* put it: 'In the opinion of many authorities on the game it was considered very doubtful whether such a feat had ever been accomplished before'. So their field's par was about 78, while 72 was not likely to occur again in either that Championship or any other. Yet a fancied competitor who took 84 was thought to have incurred no more than 'a serious handicap to winning the Championship'.

Today, of course, no one would have any hopes even of qualifying for the last 36 holes had he amassed so horrendous a total. I think, however, we can see this level of scoring in a truer light if we consider one particular comment on J.H. Taylor's play at one hole. He hit two 'very good' shots at the long 16th and followed them up with a brassie to the green. It is fair to say then that golfers of excellence had to struggle to reach a long four hole in two shots and normally expected to have to pitch on and hole the putt over greens that fell considerably short of modern standards. This appears to be how Alex Herd scored so well for his 72. *The Times* remarked of him that he was 'driving a long ball . . . pitched in most deadly fashion and over and over again holed from his approach'. Well it must have been a once-in-a-lifetime round and Alex returned to more normal form the next day with 84.

Harry Vardon showed 'no falling off from his usual accurate long game but in putting he seemed very weak'. That meant 83 for Harry, and a substantial burden to carry. Nevertheless only a few had actually bettered this score. Willie Park, for instance, twice a winner of the Open, had gone round in 79, playing with 'great steadiness', a round described as 'likely to hold the field for some time'. Harry's brother Tom, now long forgotten, was also no mean player and in fact there were judges who had earlier thought him a more accomplished and talented player than Harry. He had the 'magnificent score' of 77.

What manner of course were they playing then? I have already mentioned that they were using clubs that would not propel the modern ball anything like the distance to be expected from a steel shaft and neither did the gutta percha offer the distance that a rubber core does, though, being so much less lively, it made putting and chipping far easier. Muirfield itself was not a short course by any means. Its card does not compare with a modern championship layout, but its yardages would not look much out of place elsewhere. In 1892 it had measured 5,200 yards, but in the Spring Medal of 1894 the winner had played his 'normal' game to the turn and that meant 48. But then he had done the truly unprecedented by coming home in 31. The greens committee were not aghast at the 79 total but the 31 homeward half called for stern measures. The course was lengthened by 600 yards with, as near as I can establish, the holes measuring as follows:

1	204	10	390
2	365	11	407
3	336	12	390
4	347	13	293
5	470	14	138
6	383	15	295
7	150?	16	450?
8	497?	17	330
9	365	18	382

Total yardage was about 6,200. A player would reckon to need two good woods to reach a hole of 350 yards and that even holes as short as the 13th and 15th would still need a good firm pitch to the green, rather than a putt for an eagle.

Taylor held a little more than steady in the next round for a 78 and this gave him a commanding lead of six shots over Harry Vardon, who equalled Taylor's second round. Vardon's name was little mentioned in contemporary reports, for other golfers were pursuing Taylor more closely. Compared with Taylor's halfway total of 155, Freddy Tait had 158 – having been 'rather unfortunate on the 16th for his ball entered the bunker' – D. Brown and Willie Fernie had 157, while Alex Herd had followed that astounding 72 with 84, which nevertheless secured second place for him.

In the third round Vardon's 78 gained him three shots on Taylor. With 18 holes to play in the afternoon, this was the situation. Alex Herd was again leading on 235, followed a shot behind by Taylor. Other key scores were Ben Sayers and D. Brown 238, Harry Vardon 239 and Willie Park 243.

It is a comment on the size of golf galleries of the day that a leading contender, Vardon, was followed by no one at all in his final surge towards the Open and that an estimated ten people were gathered around the 18th green to see him hole out. His round had in the end been a pursuit of J.H. Taylor who was playing a few holes ahead and was no doubt drawing the mass of attention – a hundred or so? Taylor finished in 80 for a total of 316. With only the 18th to play someone told Vardon that he needed a four to win. Vardon later said that this 382-yard hole required 'a good drive and a real good brassie to reach the green'. That green was, however, guarded by a severe bunker, faced with railway sleepers. As Harry wondered whether to go for outright victory or play short he noticed a friend, James Kay of Seaton Carew in County Durham, pointing emphatically at the ground. The advice was obviously that Harry should play short of the bunker, pitch on and two-putt for a tie and eventual playoff. He followed the advice and in due course finished with a five and the same 316 total as Taylor.

The playoff was delayed a while for both Vardon and Taylor were committed to play elsewhere first but eventually they were duly photographed in front on the clubhouse in ankle-length boots, and proceeded to the 1st tee. Vardon opened with a birdie but was then bunkered at the second, where Taylor helpfully took three putts. Harry then birdied the next for a lead of two shots, a lead which he increased on each of the next holes to the 9th to be six better than Taylor. But at the next three holes Taylor came back, gaining a shot on each. Two halves followed but Harry then took a shot more than Taylor at the 14th and 15th. At the long 16th, however, he gained a shot on Taylor for the first time since the 8th by having a five to Taylor's six. On the 18th, Vardon hit a longer drive than he had while playing his fourth round of the Championship. This time he decided to attempt to reach the green. What Mr James Kay felt about this is not recorded. If he was there, he might well have said 'I told you so'. Vardon bunkered his brassie shot. But he got out quite well and Taylor also took five. At the end of the first playoff round Vardon was at 78, Taylor 80.

That lead went with the first shot of the afternoon: Vardon had hit a cleek out of bounds into a wood. (A cleek was an iron with a narrow, almost straight face. In Britain, its nearest equivalent today is the 1 iron, or a driving iron.) Taylor then took three as did Vardon at the second attempt. But he was apparently not much daunted by his double bogey for he was a shot better than Taylor at each of the next three holes for a lead of three. Most of the following holes were halved until the 12th, up to which point Vardon had maintained the same lead. At this 390-yard hole Taylor went boldly for the green with his second shot, while Harry played it more cautiously to find his lead cut to two strokes. On the 13th, Vardon drove into a bunker but got out well and was able to equal Taylor's four. The 14th, 15th and 16th were all halved and the

Championship was now in Harry's pocket – barring the unexpected. He then holed a 12-yard putt for a birdie which sent him happily to the last tee with a lead of three.

After each had driven there was the problem of the sleeper-faced bunker and the enticing green beyond to be faced again. This time, Vardon did as James Kay had advised him earlier and played short of it. Taylor had no such option. His one hope was to go for the green now and hope to single-putt and pray that Harry might take a six in the meantime. For an instant or so it looked as if his brassie shot was on its way to swing the playoff in his direction. But it caught the lip of the bunker and toppled in. Taylor found he could only play out sideways and in the end it was a six for Taylor and a five for Vardon who, at the age of 26, had won his first Open.

It was the beginning of an era dominated by three men: Taylor, Vardon and, (a few years later) James Braid, who joined them as final member of the 'Great Triumvirate'. After the First World War, all three were too old for great things any longer to be expected of them, though each occasionally caught fire. But in that phase between 1894 and 1914 they won the Open 16 times: five to Taylor, five to Braid and six to Vardon. The latter's record is unlikely to be beaten, for, although the Triumvirate were almost certainly as good as the best of today, there are certainly now far higher numbers of high-class players and the greatest of them, Jack Nicklaus, has won the Open twice only.

The three ages of the golfer: Severiano, Miller, Nicklaus

Each year the British Open seems to answer a number of questions, one of which is always: will Nicklaus win? The answer to that one is, almost invariably, no. The pre-post favourite, with monumental consistency finishes in second place or, in a very bad year, third. No one begins to rival his record of high finishes, yet many have won it more often than the two victories that Nicklaus can claim. To win a third time is, he says, one of the ambitions that keeps him playing golf.

Established as second favourite was Johnny Miller. You could not get better than about 7-1 on him and again there was a question:

is Miller really a great golfer, fit to take over the aura of Jones in his day, or Cotton, Nelson, Snead, Hogan, Player, Palmer, Locke and Nicklaus in theirs? You and I probably have no doubt at all, for did not Miller prove himself with his dominance of the US tournament circuit in 1974, and early in 1975, and by that lowest of all open-winning rounds, 63, at Oakmont in 1973? Well, not to everybody's taste. If you choose to rate a player by his record in major championships, Miller's did not convince; he had fought out a couple of Masters and finished second in the British Open in Tom Weiskopf's year, 1973 – a few weeks after that he snatched the US Open; that was about all. And History is a stern judge.

Only the winners of major championships are remembered and the tournament-winning runs of an Alf Padgham on the British circuit in 1936 or Horton Smith in the US several years earlier have become sadly a minor footnote in golf history. They created intense interest at the time but as the years pass all is forgotten. That a player won the Doral Eastern Open in 1962 or the Dunlop Metropolitan in 1938 informs us that he was obviously a goodish sort of a player that far-off tournament week – if you should chance to come across that particular item of information, and unless you are an aficionado you will not.

So in July 1976 Miller's claim to lasting fame was a single major-championship victory to set against the totals run up by such as Player, Jones, Nicklaus, Locke, Snead, Hogan and so on. And Miller, the Golden Boy, was 29 years old in 1976. Bobby Jones retired a year younger.

Age was indeed to be a factor in this Championship from the beginning in the person of Severiano Ballesteros who, at 19 years of age, figured throughout the four days.

But there were others to set the course on fire – in fact the Championship itself did literally threaten to go up in flames on the first day when a blaze broke out and thrived near the 1st green. The weather, as at Carnoustie the previous year, had been most untypical for Britain, both at Royal Birkdale and everywhere else, and the condition of the course was to have its effect on the ebb and flow of the Championship.

Many players, for example, are happier when hitting tee shots into soft fairways for they then know that, although the ball may not run far and they may have to hit long shots into the green, at least a good drive stays more or less where it has been put. But at Birkdale you could by no means be sure. An impeccably-straight drive could pitch against an undulation and then angle off sharply into the rough. As a result, there was a tendency for many of the competitors to take an iron from the tee to keep it on the fairway. In his last round, for instance, Miller did not use a wood from the tee until late on when he was sure he would be champion and decided to enjoy himself.

The rough itself was by no means lush and clinging but, unlike at Carnoustie, it did pose problems, and *populus albus* lurked in waiting as well. *Populus albus* is willow scrub, and if a golf ball gets into it a player may as well give up hope: he is unlikely to find it, and if he does, almost certainly he will decide that he had better pick the thing out under a one-shot penalty.

But it was the greens that caused the most consternation. Most of them were a dappled brown and green and the players did not like them at all. Few would blame them, for next door to Birkdale they could see the emerald green of what the Hillside club had produced for people to putt on. There the staff had decided that although it would probably rain on the morrow they had better pour on a few million gallons now, just to be on the safe side. But Birkdale was the scene of an Open and in both Britain and America it is considered that players must be tested by fast greens. So Birkdale was watered relatively little and its greens were seared by the sun.

To make matters worse for the first round the pins were usually set in the middle of a brown patch. For anything more than a short putt it was highly difficult to judge pace, for the ball had first to travel over a fast brown area, then across a green one before reaching the area around the hole when unpredictable things could, and did, happen.

Take for instance the case of Tom Weiskopf. Having watched a fellow competitor stroke his approach putt along exactly the same line he had no doubts about the borrow. One floats it out a few inches to the right and watches it curl gradually leftwards and, hopefully, precisely into the middle of the hole. Weiskopf struck his putt at the right pace and his ball drifted predictably towards the centre of the hole, and then twitched away uphill. Weiskopf, usually all manly charm during his visits to Britain, though renowned for petulance in the United States, was quite brusque in his opinions of the Birkdale greens when he reached the Press tent that first day.

One had to sympathise with him. Seldom can so many putts have failed to collapse at their last gasp into the hole, but instead to wriggle their way past. Nicklaus, for example, putted aggressively and well through each round. Again and again he stood poised to grin as the ball dropped and again and again he had to walk past the hole and hope he could get the thing in *this* time. His composure still held even when an exactly-judged little pitch and run seemed to descend into the hole and an unseen hand lobbed it out again. Golfers often have some cause to think that Providence is against them on the putting green and none more so than Nicklaus that week.

But, despite the condition of the greens and the willow scrub, there was compensation in the fact that Birkdale was playing short. If one looked back through the records for championships held there since it was first used in 1954 the winning scores were not low:

1954	Peter Thomson	283
1961	Arnold Palmer	284
1965	Peter Thomson	285

Then Trevino had tamed it in 1971 with 278. This year the players felt that something better than that would be needed and that there would be 66s in abundance. The Open record might well go if the winds did not blow.

All the first day there was no more than a breeze, but even this played havoc with many players' cards. Combined with a temperature in the mid-80s, the easterly dried out even further greens already parched, and the brown patches spread with a rapidity that could almost be observed from moment to moment. One who must surely have been more disconcerted than the average was Bobby Cole of South Africa who had come close to winning at Carnoustie in 1975. On the 1st hole he lagged his approach putt up to about four feet. He needed four more putts before his ball finally consented to get itself into the hole. That sort of thing takes the starch out of one's stride.

The early starters had the best of it and none more so than Christy O'Connor Junior. O'Connor said that he had played so well he could have shot 60. As it was he got halfway to that target by reaching the turn in 30. Unlike Cole, his moment of truth was not on the greens. Off the fairway on the 13th his ball came to rest against a tree root; he then hit a branch on the backswing and missed the ball. A little later on there were three putts and an eight to go down on the card. Nevertheless, this man who had hit the first shot of the Championship led from that moment on, finishing with a 69 and a new course record.

Two others with names even less known on the world stage scored equally well. One was a Japanese, Norio Suzuki. On the 16th he sent in a putt of about 12 yards to go three under par and on the 18th tee stood at four under, thus needing a par at a hole which many had birdied to lead with a 68. He drove into a bunker, came out well but then left his long iron to the green short. He pitched to about three yards and then missed the putt for a six. Never mind, that was still the joint lead. What did Norio think about it all? Difficult to say. This was the 24-year-old Japanese's first trip abroad and his only English was the rather non-golfing sentence 'all officers must work'. However, an interpreter helped him get a bit nearer to the point and then off he went to use his native language in an interview for Japanese TV, rewarded with a leader when covering the British Open for the first time.

The other first-round leader, Severiano Ballesteros, had been around in European golf for long enough to have picked up a more varied turn of phrase and it was obvious he had no illusions about his eventual prospects. He thought he would take 80 the next day if the wind got up.

These were then the three success stories but following closely were other fancied players:

70   Brian Barnes, Tom Kite, Jack Newton
71   Graham Marsh
72   Gary Player, Hubert Green, Johnny Miller

73   Tom Weiskopf, Tony Jacklin, Jerry Pate
74   Jack Nicklaus, Peter Oosterhuis, Hale Irwin

Some had fared sadly. After Gene Sarazen had a hole in one at Troon's Postage Stamp in 1973, thus rounding off 50 years of campaigning in British Opens, he had said that would be his last Championship. But here he was again, playing with two former champions, Bobby Locke and Fred Daly. Gene played only the first nine holes and then picked up, being six over level fours. At the other end of the age scale a young British hopeful, Sam Torrance, who had won a couple of tournaments earlier in the season, was rewarded by being sent out with Miller and Newton. His was an embarrassing round as more than one drive soared away to the right. At one point Miller and Newton did not quite observe the courtesies: they left him to walk back to the tee and try to hit the next one a bit better, and played out the hole as a twosome. I hope they greeted him kindly when eventually he caught them up. And, though whichever of Newton and Miller was marking Sam's card could hardly have been in a position to verify his score personally, Sam's 82 was probably believable enough.

The second day the wind did not get up but Ballesteros dropped shots to the turn. It looked as if, as usual, an unknown was rapidly backing out of the unfamiliar limelight. But he came zipping back over the last nine. By the 16th he stood minus four for the holes played and then let fly a huge drive on the 17th. Such driving was by now becoming recognized as a feature of his play. The young Spaniard threw everything into the shot. He wanted to hit the ball a long way. If indeed it should happen (and it did) to go a long way in not quite the right direction he would stalk it down in confidence that more of the same would blast the ball out of rough, bunker and undergrowth. As long as there is a crowd available to help you find the thing it is not a bad strategy. And by now Severiano was pulling them in. Here was a first-round leader that people were beginning to think might still be there on the final day.

After that zestful drive on the 526-yard 17th, Severiano felt he needed only a 3 iron for his shot into the green. He sent it to the right edge and was faced with a very long putt indeed. He ran his ball up to the hole and almost in. Never mind, that was still a birdie and he went to the 18th hole, another par five, at five under par. There followed what was said to be the longest drive of the day at that hole and this time he selected a 5 iron for the shot to the green. It was on line for the flag the whole way and there was a three-yard putt for an eagle but it did not quite go in. Severiano had a final birdie then, and a two-round total of 138 – six under par.

But Miller also had finished 4, 4 earlier in the day for a 68, compiled in more cautious a manner. He relied greatly on his 1 iron, using it no less than ten times, six of these for tee shots in preference to wood. Afterwards he commented that, apart from the putter, he thought it the most important club of the lot for playing Birkdale. Gary Player had said much the same thing two years before after taking the Open at Royal Lytham and St Anne's.

Four strokes off the lead at 142 were Hubert Green, who had won three tournaments in a row that year in the US, and O'Connor. Then, a shot behind, came Brian Barnes, Tommy Horton and Ray Floyd before a cluster of fancied players on 144 – Nicklaus, Marsh, Newton, Suzuki, Player, Pate and Kite amongst them. On that total also was Carl Higgins, a US teaching professional who surprised even himself by improving by ten shots on his first round score with a 67. This was a memorable round for Carl at least, for few watched him and there were other individual shots in plenty to savour. Tony Grubb, for instance, was just playing out his round, all hope of qualifying long gone. From the 17th tee he hit a poor drive which gave him no chance of reaching the green and took a 3 wood to cover some of the 280 remaining yards. It ran into the hole for an albatross two. As Grubb said, 'It was a good ending'. However, for him it was back to his home at Ross-on-Wye, where he concentrates on apple-growing, for he still finished five shots worse than the 152 qualifying score.

Masters champion Ray Floyd played a shot of more significance to the Championship at this same hole. His tee shot lay in light rough 230 yards from the green and he felt that he would reach with a 4 iron as the ball would fly with little backspin from the fluffy kind of lie he had. It did, to about five yards of the pin. Down went the putt for an eagle and after a birdie at the last he was round in 67, nine shots better than his opening round.

Perhaps the most dazzling burst of the whole Championship was produced by David Graham. After a first round of 77 and a poor first half in the second his thoughts must have been tending towards matters such as whether he should catch an evening flight back to the US. However, the Australian birdied five of the last six holes for a 70 and although he eventually finished out of the top 20 there was a new bounce in his stride. No doubt encouraged, he not long after won a tournament on the US circuit and later produced arguably the greatest matchplay performance ever in winning the Piccadilly: never ahead until, suddenly, he had won each successive match.

For the third day the weather was cooler and there was a period of lashing rain. Ballesteros was paired with Miller, a severe test of his temperament, and perhaps of Miller's too. Ballesteros began by hitting the 1st green in two and then three-putted, whereas Miller chipped and putted for a four. Both took fives at the 423-yard 2nd and when Miller parred the next to the Spaniard's five the pair were level for the Championship. On the 212-yard 4th, Miller came close to holing in one, but Severiano managed his first par of the round after missing the green but pitching dead with his second shot. Both parred the next and then faced what was for the whole field the most difficult hole in the course, the 468-yard 6th.

In his 1961 Open victory, for instance, Arnold Palmer did not once reach the green in two shots. It is a dogleg right with a cross bunker, followed by a ridge in the landing area of a good tee shot. If you clear both of these, you then have an undemanding pitch to the green. For most, however, the bunker is too much of a threat and players took an iron and played short of it. But they only postponed trouble, for from this position the second shot is blind – over the ridge to a green set in a fold in the sand dunes, protected by bunkers and, worse, with a clump of thick bushes on the right. Both took fives and when Ballesteros failed to par the next he found himself in the sad position of having dropped four shots in the seven holes played. Miller rubbed it in by birdieing the next, at which point he led the Spaniard by two. Severiano seemed to have made matters worse when he pushed his drive from the 9th tee into deep rough but his power enabled him to thrash it out and forwards to the green.

Ballesteros   38
Miller   34

'Ah, well,' they were all saying, 'we knew it couldn't last.' Not
a few were pleased about Severiano's decline. The British have
long become immune to the pain of having Americans, Australians
and South Africans inevitably winning the Championship, but the
prospect of having a 19-year-old Spaniard taking the title was
highly unattractive. Surely Miller would now put the stripling in
his place. Not so. Severiano immediately took his first birdie, but
followed that riposte by hooking so extravagantly from the next
tee that he had to enquire in what direction his ball had departed.
He was given the correct route and found it in a good lie, and was
on in two. Miller had hit a perfect drive, but then pushed his iron
and could not get down in two more. Level again.

Severiano needed another splendid recovery at the 184-yard
12th. Judgment awry, he sent his tee shot soaring beyond the
green and the dunes which back it, but pitched deftly to a yard
and was able to equal Miller's conventional three. At the par-three
14th, Miller pushed his iron shot and Severiano was again in the
lead. From the next tee both hooked, Ballesteros viciously but once
again finding a good lie; Miller did not, so that was a par five for
Severiano and a six for the American. At the 17th the Spaniard
again drove into the rough, which by this time probably held few
if any terrors for him. On to the green went his second shot and
down the putt for an eagle that Miller could not match. Miller was
now three behind. However, all ended as it had begun with the gap
between them two shots, for Miller comfortably birdied the last, a
par five, and Severiano did not.

Well, an unknown has led the Open before for one day, and
sometimes for two, but here was the Spaniard still in contention
and he had fully proved his resilience by turning a potentially-
disastrous round into a highly-respectable one. Contrast this with
the performance of the newly-crowned US Open champion. He
went to the turn in 39 and then recorded these inglorious figures
for the last nine: 4, 8, 5, 4, 4, 7, 4, 5, 7. A monster 48 and a total
for the round of 87. Of course that was goodbye to Jerry Pate. The

most important of those remaining, from whom the winner must surely come were:

211 Ballesteros
213 Miller
215 Horton
216 Marsh, Floyd and Nicklaus
217 Kite and O'Connor
218 Barnes and Cole (a gallant comeback after those opening five putts).

The prospects for the last round were enticing: could the callow youth hold that useful lead, or would the totally-uninhibited slash of his swing find him at last too deep in rough and bush for recovery and there would suddenly be an eight or nine to go down on the card? And what of Miller? He had produced a couple of steady rounds and one of quality. Would he get the bit between his teeth and send those towering iron shots close by the flag as he had done in the 1973 US Open?

And as always there was the dominant figure of Nicklaus, who had played far less defensively than was his custom, attacking the flag rather than the safest area of the green, but who was not holing the putts that an Open champion needed. The rest of his game was in good order and Ballesteros's five-shot lead would melt fast enough if Nicklaus achieved momentum and passion.

On the same score of 216 were also Graham Marsh and Ray Floyd, the current and overwhelming Masters champion. Both had their backers. Just ahead of this threesome, glory be, there was an Englishman, besides Ballesteros and Miller the only man under par in the field. He must have gone to bed with happy thoughts of his play on the last hole – colossal drive, precise iron and one putt for an eagle.

Of those in contention that last afternoon the playing order was Nicklaus and Floyd, followed by Horton and Marsh. Then came the leaders, Ballesteros and Miller. Well ahead of all these, almost the round of the day was in progress from a first-year British professional, Mark James. He went to the turn in 33 and had the same score coming back. And the end of it all there was easily a new course record and his total of 288 gave him a barely-plausible hope of winning. In any event, it was an achievement that gave good cause for hope that the 22-year-old might one day soon be champion.

But most eyes were on the confrontation for a second day between Miller and Ballesteros. Miller said, 'I am not looking at it that he is a dog and I am going to catch him. He's a threat and I have respect for his game. He's got a lot of courage, maybe sometimes too much.' Miller went on to refer to the Spaniard's fearsome powers of recovery and in his remarks there were undertones that perhaps Severiano would not be able to keep on hacking his ball out of the long grass and onto the green for yet another day.

But the young Spaniard carried on in the same mood. From the 1st tee he hooked into willow scrub and successfully got it out, only to put it into rough to the right of the fairway. Never mind. His pitch came to rest some ten yards from the flag and inevitably down went the putt. (The verve of Severiano's driving and his brutal forcefullness from rough places earned a great deal of comment. Less recognized was the poise and rhythm of his putting stroke.) Meanwhile, Miller had sent his tee shot straight down the fairway and followed up with a good iron shot. But the wind shifted as his ball flew at the green and eventually he finished through the back. Then there was a chip and two putts. So Severiano was now three shots to the good over Johnny Miller. Yet this was not to be the pattern of the day. Ballesteros immediately dropped a shot at the 2nd, while Miller birdied, and in a trice the margin between them was a single stroke, no sort of a cushion at all. Both proceeded to par the next three holes and confronted the 6th hole, which had all along caused trouble to the whole field and has been described earlier. It had just been causing Jack Nicklaus trouble once again. For the final day the tee markers had been set fully back and there was no chance of anyone carrying the cross bunker. Jack put a 3 wood short and had then taken out a 1 iron. 'Oh no,' he said. His ball was in a clump of bushes and Jack was perhaps too proud to look for it. A cursory glance or two and he dropped another ball under penalty of stroke and distance and managed a six. Before that he had been two under par for the round and had perhaps laid the foundation of a dominant last round. Although Jack played steadily thereafter and had birdies on three of the four par fives he made up no ground on the leaders.

Minutes later Ballesteros was in the same bushes and for him the result was much the same – a six and Miller a shot in the lead. The 8th saw the Spaniard's hopes slip further. Miller pitched dead for a birdie while Severiano was away amongst the dunes and had to accept a five. Miller three ahead, a margin few would think he would surrender for he thrives on leading, when he tends to play with increasing confidence and aggression. But still he relied on his 1 iron from the tee; again and again he was rewarded by lies near the centre of the fairways.

However, the Spaniard was not quite done for and clawed back a stroke when he birdied the 10th. But that was the end of it. Ballesteros lashed his drive at this 415-yard hole into willow scrub, found it, moved it a foot or two and then took two more before reaching the green. Once there he took three putts and Miller's four saw him into a lead of no less than five shots. Miller followed up with a birdie and an eagle and that was definitely that – inconceivable that Miller would outdo Palmer or Littler (Arnold Palmer lost a seven-stroke lead over Billy Casper over the last nine holes of the 1966 US Open; Gene did the same thing in the 1977 US PGA at Pebble Beach) and surrender so formidable a lead over the closing holes. Miller's eagle was accomplished memorably. On the 505-yard 13th he was just off the green in two and chipped in. There is always an element of luck in this, just as to hole a vast putt is to be favoured perhaps unduly by the gods, but Miller's running shot was perfect in judgment of pace and line. It always looked as if it *ought* to go in and go in it did.

Miller could now afford to be benevolent about Severiano's achievements and encourage him towards getting second place, for there was no longer the possibility that the Spaniard could catch up. He smiled as Severiano holed a long putt on the next for a birdie, though this technically did reduce the margin between them by a shot. Miller knew he was the winner and wanted to finish in style. For the first time he left his 1 iron in the bag and used his driver – into a bunker, and then pushed his third shot into another, from which he recovered nervelessly to a yard of the hole and down went the putt. On this hole, Severiano had decided to follow the maestro of the day's example. He used an iron from the tee – and pushed his shot into the rough. No, there was no way Severiano could stay on the fairway. But he gripped the club low, settled himself quickly and forced the ball somewhere near the green. He settled for a par five, as had Miller.

With the race for the title settled, another began. Ballesteros had to put in a very strong finish indeed for anything better than fifth place. He parred the 16th, which gained him no ground, and that not without difficulty for he missed the green with his approach but got down in two from a bunker. On the 17th, Severiano was for once in centre fairway and his approach to this par five settled some four yards from the hole. In went the putt for an eagle and he could look for something better than fifth place now.

The cockpit of the 18th green lay ahead, with thousands ranked in the stands for the grand climax. Miller had found the fairway and followed with a mid iron to three yards. Severiano, from light rough, pulled his second shot onto a hump to the left of the green. Miller strode through the throng, putter held in triumph on high. Then the cheers sounded for the Spaniard, who looked no more than his 19 years and decidedly shy. In the eventual silence he faced the problem of getting down in two more to tie with Jack Nicklaus for second place. Float it up in the air with a sand wedge and hope to stop it close to the hole? Or run it low along the ground between the bunkers? Severiano chose the second course and there was a roar as his ball ran smoothly and stopped four feet from the hole. Miller's turn now. He putted to about two inches and there was now a problem of etiquette: the new champion should play the last shot. But I like to think that Miller felt it appropriate for young Severiano to have the last word; he walked after his putt and tapped it in flinging his ball to the crowd, a habit he had developed over the closing holes.

The last shot was to be played by Severiano and was a stiffer task than Miller had faced. But his putting stroke held up and in it went.

It has often been said that no one remembers who finished second and in the end this was emphatically Miller's Championship, forming as it did a unique double with his US Open victory three years before. Then his final 63 was the lowest winning final round and also the lowest round played in the US Open. At Birkdale, with a 66, he had done it again: the lowest last round of a British Open winner and, indeed, only a single stroke worse than the Open record held since 1934 by Henry Cotton, with 65, and equalled by Jack Newton in 1975 at Carnoustie. Certainly Miller's victory, by six clear shots, will be remembered for a good few decades yet but so, I think, will Severiano Ballesteros's contribution to the occasion. No one so young since Young Tom Morris in the 1860s has come so close to winning the Open, nor indeed has anyone who had started a championship week known only to the cognoscenti.

Postscript

As far as I know, Ben Hogan visited Britain just three times. Each visit contributed to the legend of a man who played almost all his golf within the boundaries of the United States.

In 1949 he was crushed in a road accident. They said he would never play golf again but as he struggled to walk he was appointed captain of the US Ryder Cup team. There was no question of his playing in the match – the appointment was perhaps more of a gesture to the greatness of a man who in all probability would never play a competitive round of golf again. Moreover the encounter at Ganton was not likely to be unduly demanding on the talents of the US team: on American soil two years before the result had been USA 11, GB 1, the most crushing defeat for Britain in the history of the Cup.

The British were fatalistic about the event. Leonard Crawley, at the time the most authoritative writer on the British golfing scene, suggested that 18-year-old Peter Alliss ought to play. At least he would be blooded and there was no possibility other than that the US would win overwhelmingly. Yet Ben Hogan had to do his fair share of captaining before the US ran out as narrow 7-5 victors.

For Hogan, this was the beginning of a ride into golfing legend. Everyone has heard how the following year he decided that he might just be able to force his body around a golf course the necessary four times and appeared for the Los Angeles Open. He propelled himself to such effect that he won it, tied with Sam Snead who, alas for fairy tales, took the playoff.

But Hogan was on his way and, despite the aches and pains, was a far greater golfer than he had been before. He had taken much longer than most to reach the top but at the time of his collision with a Greyhound bus had won the US PGA twice and the 1948

US Open. After the accident, he took the US Open three years out of the next four. Why this should have happened is almost impossible to tell almost 30 years on. Perhaps it was that the furious lash of his swing had to be moderated, or the spur of having to subdue not merely the opposition but also his damaged body. Hogan himself thought that it was more to do with alterations of method moving the right hand more over the shaft and weakening the left-hand grip, all of which, he felt, curbed his tendency to hook.

Whatever the truth of the matter, in 1953 he took the US Masters, followed that with the US Open and then made up his mind after urgings from such as Walter Hagen and Gene Sarazen to attempt the British Open for the first time. With a kind of inevitability he tamed both Carnoustie and his caddie: 'When I want you to talk I'll speak to you.' The following year Hogan did not defend and as the years have passed he has refused invitation upon invitation to make a sentimental journey to compete once again. Hogan has always felt that he will only play in any event if there is the prospect of winning. He does not aim to number himself amongst those figures of the golfing past who perennially start the US Masters off and then slip away from the course after nine holes, or make up a threesome of former British Open winners who relaxedly stroll around before failing to qualify for the third round.

No, Hogan played to win – today he is seen no more in competition, though still he relishes a remote corner of a practice ground and the striking of a golf ball to the precise destination he has ordained for it.

It was, for Hogan, the putting that went. A man that was reckoned by his contemporaries to be the best man around with a centre shaft became first ordinary, then poor and, finally, tortured. Perhaps this is why he once rasped at Billy Casper, at that time much underestimated as a swinger of a golf club, 'if you couldn't putt, you'd be selling hot dogs outside the ropes'.

But after his 1953 British Open victory, which completed the only rival achievement to Bobby Jones's Grand Slam of 1930, Hogan played competitively in Britain only once more.

Jones won the British and US Amateur and Open Championships. He could not win the US PGA because as an amateur he was not qualified; neither could he win the US Masters because in this case he had not invented the Tournament. Hogan, as a professional, was not qualified for the two amateur events Jones won, and because of a clash of dates had to choose between the British Open and the US PGA.

The occasion was the Canada Cup, since renamed the World Cup. On the first day there was very little wrong with his short game. In that June of 1956 at Wentworth he began by holing a 12-yard chip on the 1st and followed with a putt of about four yards. On the 4th he got one in from the edge of the green. After a conventional par on the next his card read: 3, 2, 4, 3, 3. Nothing much went wrong for the rest of the outward half and he then came to the par-three 10th, arrowed the ball into the green and then knocked in a six-yard putt for a two.

So far, it was all very like Bobby Jones's return to St Andrews for a friendly game in 1936. On that occasion, the masses had gathered to see a legend and the legend had not failed them. Neither, in 1956, did Hogan, followed by about half the total gallery. As he marched, inscrutable as usual, to the 11th tee he was no less than seven under level fours. Thereafter, the great man was fallible. From the 11th tee he was bunkered and took three putts. On the next, he misjudged his approach shot and was short, then hit his next too firmly; suddenly, he had used 11 strokes on two holes against a strict par of eight. (Any professional or amateur of high class feels that he ought to reach the green of any par five in two shots, unless hitting into a headwind; in this sense the card par of a course may be, for example, 72, but if this includes four par fives, we should reckon the 'strict' par at 68.) Although the ultimate magic was gone, Hogan thereafter played finely, though taking three putts on the 15th green, and signed his card for a 68. His partner, Sam Snead, was eight shots worse.

The pattern was similar as day followed day. Each time, Ben Hogan went to the turn near faultlessly and scored much less well coming home. Meanwhile, Snead had burdened the US team score with 76, 73 and these were the two greatest players of their country. It must be embarrassing to record 76, 73 when your partner is living out his legend with 68, 69.

Let us leave them there for the moment, for the careers of Ben Hogan and Sam Snead tell us a very great deal about greatness and what is memorable in golf history. For example, Sam Snead and

Roberto de Vicenzo have won more tournaments than anyone else, though Gary Player is in close contention. But who cares? As time passes Roberto will be remembered most for winning, at long last, the British Open in 1967 and for signing his card for the wrong score in the US Masters the next year. Snead will be remembered for arguably the most rhythmic of all golf swings and a comic series of disasters in the US Open which has left him comfortably the greatest player never to have won it. And what of Hogan? In the modern era he stands on a level shared only by Jones, Palmer, Nicklaus and . . .? His place in the Hall of Fame is secure and yet it rests on a relatively short space of time. That space is a brief period dating from a vague point at which he stopped hooking destructively and instead faded the ball gently and, only a little more than five years later, began to be a rather poor putter. But that five years is enough. No one feels at all confident in stating that Jack Nicklaus is not the greatest of them all, but once that hurdle is over, it is then easy enough to say that either of Jones or Hogan is the all-time number one.

Back now to Wentworth on 26 June 1956. In the third round, Hogan went out in 33 but played the second half relatively weakly to record a 72. In the team event the US position improved, for Snead was playing solidly now on a course that held no happy memories for him: it was he who, in the 1953 Ryder Cup, had his match against Harry Weetman palpably sewn up and then pro-ceeded to strike a stream of tee shots deep into the woods.

At lunchtime, the US team stood at three shots worse than Canada, represented by the best team they have fielded – Stan Leonard and Al Balding. Thereafter the Canadians wilted, or perhaps it was far more that the US star was irresistibly in the ascendant. Difficult indeed, except for club golfers, to imagine a three-stroke lead become a 16-stroke deficit but that is in fact what happened. At the end of the day, after what is claimed to be a record slow round of five hours 15 minutes (surely plenty of people have taken longer than that since?), the USA had come from behind and were quite overwhelmingly victorious. It should be no surprise to those who like their legendary figures to conform to their image that Mr Hogan totalled 277 for the four rounds and that he was the individual winner by five shots over Roberto de

Vicenzo and by six over the effortless Belgian stylist Flory van Donck.

But for a few the memory of Hogan that lingered was not a selection of shots compiled along the West Course at Wentworth in the process of his steady advance to victory but the sight of him practising at dusk, when the toils of the day were over for most. It is said that Harry Vardon could hit brassie shots inexorably at the flag and stop them not too far off. No one was his rival in this respect. But watching Hogan you knew that here was a man who had taken the thing a long stride further. Length was the keyword. Harry did not expect to hit a brassie (call it a 2 wood if you prefer) much more than 180 yards, and from that distance there is little doubt that he very frequently did get his ball to settle near the flag. But Hogan that year at Wentworth was doing the same trick from about 100 yards further away.

But the yardages aside, it is enough to say that Ben W. Hogan played competitive golf twice only in Great Britain. At Carnoustie links in 1953 he won the Open Championship; three years later, amongst the trees of Wentworth, he won the World Championship and was careful never to play in Britain again. Legends are created that way and should not be disturbed by the frivolities that other golfers allow themselves when the days of glory are long past.

Keeping it going

It is no easy matter to play just one good round of golf and more difficult by far to do it four times to win championship or tournament. Occasionally a Jack Fleck emerges from almost total obscurity and beats a Hogan. Then, of course, he is seen no more. He has had his Shakespearian crowded hour.

But there have been a few who have managed to maintain the level of play that Jack Fleck achieved for a few days at the Olympic Country Club in San Francisco in 1955 or Francis Ouimet at Brookline more than six decades ago over the longer period of a season. As with all such generalizations, there are of course exceptions. Jack Nicklaus has had a good year every year (sometimes more and sometimes less) since he first came on the golfing scene at the beginning of the 1960s. So also did Bobby Jones between 1923 and his retirement in 1930 and Harry Vardon between 1896 and 1914.

In the chapter which follows I have mainly concentrated on what is usually called the 'hot streak', something occupying a period of weeks and months.

Annus mirabilis

We can most of us look back, alas often too far back, at a year when things went really rather well. We won two or three cups and the handicap came down to an ever-after quite unmanageable number. The glory that may still remain is that handicap of six, nine or whatever, and in consequence a great many golf balls and side bets are lost through giving too many strokes away to too many people during Sunday morning four-balls.

Golfers of more firepower than the club handicapper are similar in at least this respect. All could pick out a year that stands out in the memory above all others. For Bobby Jones it was 1930, when he took the professional and amateur championships of both Britain and the USA. Then a couple of years later Sarazen won both the British and US Opens and some 20 years later stern Hogan came to Carnoustie to sample links golf, regarded it with unconcealed distaste, but nevertheless got down to the job in hand. He returned to America with the British Open to add to his previous victories that year in the US Masters and Open, a feat not since equalled even by Nicklaus.

Most of the great ones have reluctantly recognized such peaks only when looking back in time. Golfers are nothing if not optimists: a Hiram C. Schlumberger, a Fred Brown or a Hogan alike most certainly did not know they had reached a peak; it just felt that at last they were playing their 'normal' game. The Jacklin of 1970 and the Horton Smith of 1929 must have felt much the same. They had shown just how good they were and, after ironing out a minor problem or two the next year, would be better still. That next year' failed to arrive.

A few other great golfers have had a change of fortune far more unnerving. It is as if they went to bed one night, in keen anticipation of renewed demonstrations of supremacy come the morning, but some malicious wand was waved as they slept, and overnight they were gone from the Everests of golf.

Think of George Archer. In 1969 he was the holder of the US Masters and the best putter in the world; today, and for some time, it is a very good day for George if he can break par. Or a golfer of the more distant past: Ralph Guldahl, winner of the US Open in consecutive years, 1937 and 1938; only Jones and Hogan have done that since the First World War. In triumph and disaster Guldahl *looked* the same man. He and friends, when the bad days came so suddenly, would look at film of his swing. Yes, the power and the precision were surely still there. But the trouble was that the right things were no longer happening to the ball.

Never mind. If one has been a great player, at least the memory remains. Better still though is to have been a great player for a long time. And better again to improve as the years go by and then reach a final peak, shrug your shoulders, with everything worth the winning won, and retire. Jones in 1930 did this, with all the 't's crossed and every 'i' dotted.

In amateur golf, Michael Bonallack came close to this kind of perfection in 1968. For about 15 years he was the best British amateur, though his form was by no means always on a plateau of excellence. Day in and day out, however, Bonallack was a man well worth a bet that he would get down in two from off the green, and he had also an infallible method for stuffing a vitally important putt into the hole. 'You just *will* it in,' he said. His long game was less reliable. At his best, the swing was good enough. The ball soared away with just the right amount of left-to-right fade that keeps the tee shot on the fairway and holds iron shots on the greens. But hitting a fade is only a safe shot when you are playing well. The method is subject to only marginally less disaster than the beautiful parabola of the perfect drawn shot that can become a quick, sharp hook which deceives the troubled eye of the golfer and has him asking where that one went to. When your fade goes wrong you can see it well enough. It is that ball going straight down the middle for at least 50 yards before it takes a sharp right turn and heads for wild country. There is another problem too. The fader aims for the left side of the fairway, intending to start the ball off that way and then drift gently towards the centre or right-hand side. But a slicing kind of swing, as you come into the ball from the outside, can also generate a splendidly struck, quite straight, pull far into the left rough.

But both of these are extremes of the right-to-left method. If Bonallack found his swing was off when he picked the club up too quickly and then took it back on the outside without enough body turn, the resultant shot was usually a safe enough one. It went off down the left-hand side of the fairway and drifted across too early, in mid flight rather than that just perceptible tail-off as the ball begins to think about coming back to earth.

In May of 1968 Bonallack took the English Amateur Strokeplay Championship at Walton Heath without apparent difficulty. For the three rounds, he went 69, 70, 71. True, he palpably faltered on the 11th in his final round, when the maestro of willing the thing into the hole had to exert his willpower no less than four times before the job was accomplished! But soon after he countered with a couple of birdies, when the will proved once again equal to the occasion.

And so to Troon for the major event of the amateur year, and this time it was matchplay. Nobody troubled Bonallack. In the quarter final he stood eight under par after 31 holes and thereafter dropped a shot or two before walking back to the clubhouse with a four and three victory. The semi-final also passed by with no great alarms for him. Next there was Joe Carr, Bonallack's sole rival to the title of supreme amateur of the post-war era. Indeed it would be difficult to put the case that their predecessors, Cyril Tolley and Roger Wethered, were their superiors.

Joe Carr had surpassed expectations by reaching the final. His putting had always been by far the weakest part of his game, so much so that he had been known to put his trust in a 3 iron to bumble the thing into the hole. By 1968 these days were past but there was an even more direct problem to contend with. It had been a long, hard week and Joe Carr was 46 years old. By lunch it seemed all over. Bonallack was six up after the first round and although Carr held him in the afternoon Bonallack eventually won by the ponderous margin of seven and six. For Bonallack this was the first of a string of three victories in the Amateur. John Ball, with eight victories between 1888 and 1912, is well ahead of Bonallack's five successes but none of these was consecutive.

Bonallack then went to Carnoustie for the British Open. There were a few who hoped, rather than believed, that just possibly he might be the first amateur to win it since Bobby Jones. But in the last 40 years very few amateurs, even those who play just as much golf as any professional, have come at all close to winning an open or the US Masters. The names of Frank Stranahan, Ken Venturi, Marty Fleckman and the Jack Nicklaus of 1960 do come to mind, and also the daring Billy Joe Patton of the fast backswing and much faster downswing who, with victory becoming probable, went for long carries over water at Augusta. The first time his 4 wood finished in Rae's Creek, as it fronted the 13th green and then into the pond at the 15th. That was the end of him, but when it was all over and they came to say 'back luck', he had the grace to make one of the most imperishable of golfing remarks about his disappointment: 'Hell, it ain't like losing a leg!'

Bonallack began well. An opening 70 gave him the joint leadership. Thereafter he played well but not well enough. A total of 300 left him 11 shots behind Gary Player, the winner, but there were many great names with worse scores than Bonallack's and he finished as the leading amateur. Another silver medal.

Of the golfing season in Britain, only the English Amateur Championship now remained. Bonallack was the holder and had won it four of the six previous years. He came to Ganton, one of the very best of British inland courses, as the hottest favourite in years. But Bobby Jones never conquered his fears of what can happen over the brief 18 holes of matchplay and Bonallack had to start fast seven times and keep going before reaching the calmer waters of a 36-hole final.

In the first round he had a bye and then overwhelmed his first two opponents by six and five and five and four. On the Thursday of that championship week, quarter and semi-finals' days, he began not to know where the ball was going – the slice to the right fairway, or the finely struck pull to the left rough? On the whole, he managed to hit shortish, cutty little ones to finish on the right of the fairways. In the morning he came through by two and one, and in the afternoon met Peter Hedges. Hedges played the prettier golf – Bonallack was the man who was getting the putts in and was usually down in two from off the green. On the 16th Bonallack, one up at the time, hit another bad drive but was in no trouble. Hedges pulled from the tee into the rough, could not reach the green and that was Bonallack dormie two and goodbye Peter, see you next year.

Bonallack, the Master showing signs of being a far lesser mortal, had to meet Gordon Clark, one of an endless succession of fine Northumberland golfers, the next morning. Bonallack had three birdies in the first five holes, which meant he could look forward to a relaxed lunch. The match ended on the 15th.

In the afternoon he met Michael Attenborough, an international who had been playing very well indeed. Attenborough's drive suddenly left him and after nine holes he was five down. He then took the 10th but at the next Bonallack 'willed' a winning putt into the hole once again. It was the fifth time that he had single-putted a green. Attenborough then found his game and took the next three holes, but it was too late in the day. One good shot only would finish him. At the 250-yard 17th hole Bonallack duly hit one right at the flag. The next day he would meet David Kelley in the 36-hole final.

Over 18 holes everyone accepts that just about anything can

happen but 36 holes can be counted on to produce the best man on the day. Over a stretch of this length you can ignore your opponent and settle for par golf. That anyway was the strategy that David Kelley decided on. He was, of course, fully aware of Michael Bonallack's reputation but a couple of 71s over Ganton's 6,905 yards should be good enough. Kelley thought he could do that.

Although it is a lot more difficult to play par golf than decide that is what you want to do, Kelley managed to carry out the master plan for 13 holes. At that point he was seven down. While he strove to ignore Bonallack and follow Bobby Jones's saying, 'I'll settle for par any time', Bonallack had collected seven birdies and an eagle. He had gone out in 32 and had then begun to improve. At the 173-yard 10th he hit a 6 iron to about three yards and inevitably holed the putt. At the 11th, a driver, followed by a 9 iron, left him a couple of yards away and that was another birdie. The same clubs were used at the next hole and again the putt went down. Now for the 507-yard 13th. He needed a 3 wood for his second shot here and had a six or seven-yard putt left. That was the eagle.

By now Mr Kelley felt that he could do little more than stand and watch. In fact, Bonallack played a little less well on the way back to the clubhouse. The 14th at Ganton measures a mere 288 yards. Bonallack had only a par there and on the next he missed the green with a 5 iron and then floated a sand wedge all of five yards away from the hole. But the putt still went in. Nevertheless, a scrambled par was a little out of keeping with the majesty of his progress. On the 16th Bonallack was himself again. On this 456-yard hole he struck a 5 iron to 18 feet or so and that was another birdie. For the last eight holes played he stood at seven under par. But now (never mind poor Kelley any more) there was a final pressure to face. He had never broken the magic 30 over nine holes on any occasion, friendly or otherwise. He needed to par the 250-yard 17th and the 448-yard final hole to do so. A 3 wood to the 17th green and two putts meant that one safely past, and then a good drive went safely between the trees at the last to the ideal position for the shot into the green. 'Will a 7 iron be enough?', he asked his caddie. Though Bonallack's ball did reach the green, it was at least 20 yards short of the hole and his approach putt finished a couple of yards away.

Never mind, the fairy story was not spoiled. The putt went in and there was the magic 29 and a total for the round of 61, ten under par.

Perhaps a regret or two remained. That 12-foot putt at the 8th nearly went in, and a 6 iron at the last might well have finished a lot nearer the hole. Indeed it had not been a perfect round. Bonallack had missed four greens. Perhaps he could improve in the afternoon.

But by this time there was not much golf left in the match, unless Bonallack had decided to see how well he could knock the ball along with his umbrella. In fact, Kelley had a moment of glory on the 5th where, following the keeping-to-par strategy, he won the hole. Two more holes and it was all over, by 12 and 11.

There has never been a greater margin of victory in the English Amateur and only a couple of times in the British Amateur. The nearest comparison is with Lawson Little's annihilation of Wallace by 14 and 13 in 1934, for the winner had figures nearly comparable with Bonallack's. After 23 holes Little had taken 82 shots which, for those of us with statistical interests, is 3.565 strokes per hole. Bonallack's average was 3.56. Better by a whisker.

The 1968 season had only one thing left worth playing for in amateur golf: the US Amateur Championship. If Bonallack could take that, it would be the climax to the greatest year of golf played by an amateur since Bobby Jones. And it was to be played at Scioto Country Club, Columbus, Ohio, where Jones in his time had won the US Open. There was that morsel of golfing history to urge Bonallack on, but little else. For example, two British golfers have taken the US Open since the First World War – Ted Ray in 1920 and Tony Jacklin exactly 50 years afterwards. The last time a Briton won the US Amateur was 1911, when Harold Hilton had rather a scrambling victory.

Bonallack stirred hopes at the end of the first round when he held the lead. A few more British pressmen scurried across the Atlantic to see history made. Bonallack kept going well but not well enough. In the end the Championship was fought out between 19-year-old Bruce Fleisher and Vinny Giles. Giles put together one of the final rounds of a lifetime to finish with a 65 and a total of 285. Fleisher was one shot better. On the final day Bonallack still had a chance, but though he went round steadily the chips were not quite close enough and the putts did not make that reassuring sound of toppling into the hole. No sixes on the card but nothing inspiring either. Bonallack finished at 296 and that was good enough for 11th place only.

Still, as that song puts it, it had been a very good year.

What then made Michael Bonallack so great an amateur golfer? Well, for a start he played, and plays, all his golfing life as an amateur when most British players, especially in recent years, have seen a Walker Cup team place as an instant passport to the rewards of professional golf. Yet whereas a Ben Crenshaw or Jerry Pate have been able to transfer immediately from the role of top amateur to outstanding professional, British players have almost invariably proved incapable of doing so. Perhaps Mark James and Nick Faldo will prove to be exceptions and certainly their performances in the 1976 British Open were a good deal more than promising. But whatever the successes and failures of the British amateur-turned-pro they are lost to the amateur game. If they fail to make it to the summits then they settle for the more comfortable routines of the club professional.

So Bonallack, in deciding not to opt for professional golf, had time on his side to build his total of five wins in the British Amateur and five in the English Amateur. He was runner up just once, in itself a clue to the reasons for the man's successes: he was a good golfer, but a far better *competitor*. If Bonallack's swing was in sound working order, he was unexcelled by any professional at the intangibles of thinking and trying. This was especially noticeable as he putted. The feet would straddle wide over the ball and Bonallack then stooped low, with nose almost touching the end of the shaft, almost as if he were sniffing the whereabouts of the ball. The preparations made, he would then 'will' it into the hole with a consistency both distressing and depressing to his matchplay opponents. One of the results was the feat of appearing in eleven finals and winning ten of them, in itself perhaps a record.

All this may well remind you of someone – Peter Oosterhuis. Reaching the top roughly a decade later he probably paused only briefly before deciding that the talents of a Bonallack were his also, and his career to date shows us what Bonallack might have achieved, and also how the limitations might have hampered progress. Both have a suspect swing and in the harsh competition of the professional world the fade that becomes a slice and the vast push to the right, that Oosterhuis is prone to, make success distinctly less inevitable.

The best fat king for a cat to look at

No king at all in fact, except in achievement, but rather Archbishop Arthur D'Arcy Locke. 'Archbishop' was the nickname coined to reflect the measured dignity of his progress along the fairways of Britain, America and South Africa; 'Arthur' and 'D'Arcy' would not do at all for a golfer, so it had to be 'Bobby' Locke. I doubt if His Eminence, at least in the days of his greatness, was any more pleased with it than R.T. Jones Junior, who had always to be 'Bobby' to Press and Public but was 'Bob' to his friends.

But why should Locke be *the* great golfer that the cats, mice and minnows can, just about, think of emulating. Well, let us approach it from another direction. Consider the swing of Tom Weiskopf. The club moves back easily, then comes a suggestion only of a pause at the top and a slow beginning of the downswing. Most of us do not find these three elements easy to emulate. But then comes the impossible. The clubhead accelerates to a blur and away goes the ball for 300 yards or so. Or Hogan, at his physical peak weighing in at around nine and a half stone, but with whiplash in the swing. No one, of course, would ever arrive at the conclusion that they too could play like Jack Nicklaus. There is just too much evidence of massive power at work; the measured deliberation of the backswing until he has got the club to the point from which a siege-engine blow can be launched. Three contrasting swings, all utterly beyond the average golfer.

No these three, and a host of others, are athletes of the golf course. They have the conventional vice-like but easy grips which, if attempted by a club golfer, would lock his muscles so that it would become impossible to remove the clubhead from its resting place on the turf, let alone swing it back around his neck. More though, they have the ability, I suspect inborn, to accelerate a clubhead to a fearsome velocity. All in all it looks as if they would have little difficulty in throwing a javelin or lobbing a discus a very respectable distance.

But Bobby Locke at his peak gave no such impression. If anything, he made the youth of Britain and America suspect that golf is the ideal pastime for any middle-aged man who can propel himself for the required five or six miles around a golf course. For a start, Bobby Locke did not have that kind of fatness of a games player no longer in hard condition. 'Flabby' was almost the word. Yet he beat the best of his day, first in South Africa, then in Britain and, most surprisingly of all, established in America a near monopoly of the winner's right hand reaching out for the prize cheque!

What then was the Locke method? Central to it was his avoidance of tension. Before playing, while executing every kind of shot, in walking the course between shots, and when the day's play was over, the fewer mentions there were of the word 'golf' the better.

Let us look first at his thoughts on swinging a club. His teaching stressed ease as opposed to force, a long backswing flowing to and through the ball as opposed to the acceleration most have attempted to generate in the last couple of feet before the ball is struck. When he first came to Britain, Locke found that he compared sadly with the British professionals of the day in the distance he could get with a tee shot. Everyone was hitting them certainly no less than about 240 yards, whereas Bobby had been used to seeing his ball come to a stop no more than 215 yards away. Twenty years later, Gary Player, in much the same situation, decided to concentrate on physical fitness and muscle building to increase his length. Not so the 18-year-old Locke. He decided to change not the force but the angle of his attack at a golf ball: almost to hook the ball instead of his customary slight fade. That way he could maintain his rhythm but the ball would roll much further.

You can still see the result in the next British Open. Locke is that man drawing a bead on the right rough, or an improbable 20 or 30 yards to the right of a green and away goes the ball to arc gently back towards the centre of the fairway or the flag. My own brightest image of him is seeing him play the pitch to the green at St Andrews for the last hole of his last British Open win in 1957. Would he, as usual, aim far to the right or in such a situation decide instead to try and hit it straight to somewhere near the green and trust to a chip and a couple of putts? No, the ball floated out to the right and curved on a string in towards the flag to finish a few yards short.

Peter Alliss – Britain's most successful golfer between the Cotton and Jacklin eras

top left Peter Thomson – winner of five British Opens
top right Jack Nicklaus – the great days are not yet over
bottom left Arnold Palmer – a characteristic finish

Gary Player – does that all-black strip absorb the sun and give him extra power?

Lee Trevino – extrovert extraordinary

Tony Jacklin – perhaps the best driver in the world, and if only the putting . . .

Brian Barnes – the man who beat Nicklaus twice in one day (1975 Ryder Cup)

Johnny Miller – at Birkdale en route to the 1976 Open title

Tom Weiskopf – the purest swing in modern golf?

A couple of putts, a par, a touch at the white peaked cap in acknowledgment of the applause, and a fourth Open Championship.

Despite this apparently routine finish, there was in fact a moment of some drama earlier in the game. Before putting, Locke had marked his ball the length of a putter head away. When, a while later, the moment came for him to take his putt, he forgot about that shift of a few inches. Peter Thomson, the runner up, quite reasonably protested and here were the seeds of one of those immortal disqualifications or penalty strokes that last in the memory. But the R and A ruled that Bobby had derived no advantage from moving his ball and that his score would stand.

Perhaps that part of the pattern, the angle of attack, would not be too difficult for a handicap golfer to achieve. Anyone can be taught to hook a ball, given a few years in the attempt. But the end result would tend to be a precarious and seldom-achieved balance between the one that kept on going to the right and the other that whipped away all too sharply to the left, mixed with a high proportion of shut-faced, smothered shots that went nowhere very far away from the striker.

No, the element in Bobby's method that everyone ought to be infected with is lack of tension. First he always stressed the simple business of holding the club: never grip the thing tightly, or indeed anything other than loosely. Bobby first sorted out his thoughts in this area with regard to putting. Early on, he realized that he might have few physical attributes of great significance, but he did at least have 'feel' in his finger tips. Relying on that feel, he became a great putter. He had outstanding judgment of the pace of a putt. This was the reason for his particular measured stroll about the green: he was trying – nearly always successfully – to get the feel of grain and the condition of the turf so that he would know in his finger tips just how hard to stroke it away; Locke was also an extremely sure holer-out from two feet and closer.

It was the same, in Locke's mind, for longer shots, and here his teaching is radically different from what most, if not all, experts have urged. Cotton, for example, declared that a golf club must be held very firmly indeed. How then to avoid stress in the arm and shoulder muscles that prevents a club being swung back smoothly and far enough? Develop very strong hands, said Cotton, so that the arm and shoulder muscles are little involved in the effort of holding on through the golf swing. He augmented the strength that any golfer must inevitably have as a result of merely playing golf, by keeping a rubber ball in his pocket and squeezing it day in and day out. Although most major golfers have probably not been quite as diligent as this, they have all felt that the club must be held very firmly indeed at the moment of impact to avoid any twisting as the ball is struck.

Undeniably this does happen if the ball is cradled in heather or clinging grass. Yet in recent years several experts in the fields of ballistics and mechanics have turned their thoughts to both the golf swing in general and what actually happens at impact in particular. With one voice they agree with Locke: if the clubface is square to the intended line of flight at the precise moment it strikes the ball, that is all that is needed. Thereafter, you can allow the thing to fly out of your hands if you like. Though your popularity with fellow golfers may suffer, your ball will remain in ignorance of what you are up to, influenced only by the alignment of your clubhead at impact.

Others have argued that it is instinctive – even if the grip is moderately gentle throughout most of the swing – for the fingers to firm up as the player nears the moment of striking. 'Conquer the instinct,' Locke would say, and believed that he had been able to do so. If that sometimes convulsive tightening were successfully avoided, the swing remained on the correct path and was not diverted from it late on in the downswing – if indeed not long before.

Peter Alliss does not, however, agree with Locke's teaching. He feels that a light grip for Locke worked because Bobby had outstanding natural balance and never during the golf swing manoeuvred himself into an 'ugly' position. Peter feels that the average golfer who is never in anything other than an ugly position and never wholly on balance would inevitably find his club flying from his loose grip if he married the Locke grip to the average golfer's convulsive heave at the ball.

Tension, for Bobby Locke, had to be completely avoided before a game. He liked to go to bed when pleasantly tired at perhaps ten in the evening and rise early, for there must be no haste in any of the everyday procedures before reaching the 1st tee. He would shave with relaxed deliberation, eat languidly, drive off to the clubhouse at funeral pace and, once there, slow down even more. Peter Alliss well remembers the way Locke got himself into his golf clothes, a process much punctuated by pauses for the telling of a story here and there while the next sock to be installed on the Locke foot dangled in his fingers. Eventually the job would be done: the habitual white shoes and white cap were suitably adjusted and the roominess of his plus fours ensured there would be none of the nagging minor discomfort of a pair of hip or thigh-hugging slacks. Locke was ready to take charge of the 6,600 yards of tee, fairway and green that was his 'archbishop's diocese' for a day.

He played his shots with little delay but again there was a ritual, albeit a brief one: a couple of gentle practice swings to get the feel of a particular club into his finger tips, and away the ball went on its curving flight from right to left. It was from this point that Locke's stately progress did cause irritation. He walked, again to keep tension at bay, with arms hanging loosely down – no harm to anyone, but very definitely *slowly*. His name became associated with the five-hour round of golf and there were frequent threats during his tournament career to penalize him for slow play. Locke argued that once he reached his ball he struck it without delay. There was not the fidgeting of feet of a Sanders or Oosterhuis. The time he lost through slow walking was made up by the relative speed of his brief preparations for hitting the ball.

Yet what was considered slowness in the Locke of the mid-1950s was a round of golf that took three and a half hours; as all club golfers know, this today is about par. Attitudes have changed for today *every* golfer spends time over *every* shot. Locke said he learned to play slowly in the United States; the club golfer learns the art from watching television. Consider this example of high-speed golf: in the 1954 Daks Tournament at Little Aston, Peter and Bernard Hunt took three hours and 53 minutes to complete their golfing chores for the day. For *two* rounds! And this was by no means a case of two professional golfers getting the job done in haste to drive or fly to X or Y. They were leading the field and at the end of the day Peter was in no hurry at all to be away. He wanted to stay to collect the cheque for first prize.

The point, however, is that as a youth Locke had made up his mind about what the rhythm of his golfing life should be and thereafter was not to be diverted from the chosen path. It suited him and he stuck to it, massively imperturbable. The pity of it was that he had not decided to stride round the course every bit as rhythmically but to a more urgent tune.

When, eventually, the round was over, Locke was still concerned with the avoidance of stress. More than anything else, he did not wish to talk about golf and particularly deplored locker and bar-room wailings from golfers who had missed this and that length of putt, had suffered bad luck in the bounce and kick of a ball – and all the other things that most of us complain about so bitterly. But Archbishop Locke was by no means inclined towards monasticism. True that, in order to preserve himself as a golfing property he smoked and drank little, but he enjoyed the exchange of stories and to sing a song, accompanying himself on a ukelele. This conviviality was in marked contrast to his demeanour on the course. When he was about his business – which is how he regarded his professional life as a golfer – Locke had words for no one. He would, like Hogan, say 'Good shot' if one sufficiently meritorious had been hit, but that was his limit. He was one of those who attempt to wrap themselves in a cocoon of concentration which he would not allow to be broken by spectators who wished later to be able to say that they had 'had a chat with Bobby Locke'. He developed a technique for dealing with the situation: do not meet the man's eyes and he may then not speak at all but, if the onslaught still looms imminent, sidestep at the last moment and escape down the fairway. Later there came a refinement, although this did involve Locke in having to speak. If the sidestep failed, he took the man gently by the elbow and said, 'I'll see you later'. The man invariably fell back satisfied – the great man had spoken to him and what was more, there was to be a meeting later. Later? And where? Golf galleries are not permitted to wander through a clubhouse looking for golfers to talk to. . . . But by the time the realization had dawned Locke had made good his escape.

Of course there was more to Locke as both man and golfer than his determined pursuit of being relaxed in mind and swing. Only Bobby Jones as an approach putter, and Walter Hagen for sinking the shorter ones, can compare, over a long period of time (anyone can hope to be a superb putter for a season or so). Locke himself feels that he missed his share of short putts but few believe him. He was happier once the distance was over, say, four feet for then his sensitivity with a putter came into play and he was always the best bet of any to hole more than his share of medium-length ones and lay the long ones close by the hole.

His touch was evident in another area too. Peter Alliss believes that, of the golfers he has seen, Locke had the best judgment of distance of them all. This meant, for example, that though Locke was underpowered, and therefore more often than most a pitch shot short of the par fives, he was then able to float it in as close to the hole as many were getting their first putts. And, of course, anyone who putts well, almost invariably is as good as a chipper. If anything, Locke's chipping was even better.

So far then the elements of Bobby Locke's game were not beyond the reach of a club golfer, at least insofar as they call for physical talents that are not substantially above those of the average golfer. All of us, for example, might well putt very much better if we did not nullify the feeling we have in our hands by grasping the club as if strangulation were the intention; if we saw putting more as a delicate matter akin to tapping a snooker ball or lobbing a dart at a board we would be more likely to get the ball somewhere near the hole. But though Locke can be taken as a model and, after diligent study, the bad golfer might become really quite good, none of us is likely to threaten Locke's record.

The foundations were laid at a precocious age. He won the South African Open for the first time in 1935, when he was 17. Before the Second World War called a halt to Locke's career, he had won it four times more. But golf in South Africa at that time was parochial. Locke had to prove himself overseas. He first came to England in 1936 and did well in his first Open, finishing seven strokes behind the winner, Alf Padgham. On his third visit in 1938 Locke was a professional and won his first tournament outside South Africa, the Irish Open. He had begun with an 80, and after two rounds the man on whom Locke had set his sights as the golfer he had to topple, Henry Cotton, had a nine-stroke lead. Locke came back at him in the third round with the lowest score of the Championship,

69, but Cotton was still five shots better with one round to go. Par for the last four holes at Portmarnock was 3, 5, 5, 5; Locke covered them in 2, 4, 4, 4 for a final round of 70 and victory by two shots as Cotton faltered. This was one of the few tournaments, apart from the Open, that Bobby had been able to enter: he had not been a professional long enough to be allowed entry according to the harsh PGA rules that remained unchanged for many more years.

A few days later came one of the most dramatic four-ball challenge matches in golf history. (Very few four-balls, I must admit, are long remembered. Can any reader recall the result of a single Ryder Cup encounter of this type – unless he happens to have been watching?) The 1937 British Open champion was paired with the 1938 winner, Reg Whitcombe, against Sid Brews and Locke over 72 holes. Although Locke managed one sequence of 27 holes in approximately 95 strokes, Cotton 'won' the match with one of golf's most remembered shots. At the 391-yard 12th hole at Walton Heath in the final round he imperiously waved the crowd back. There was a chance of reaching the green if you cared to cut across the angle of the dogleg. To do this required a drive of form-idable carry over trees. The crowd having removed themselves from the line of fire, Cotton brought the shot off, his ball coming to rest a few yards only from the putting surface. He got his next dead and that was a birdie to square the match. The British pair birdied the 13th and 15th and maintained a lead of two up until the match ended.

But Locke had played the best golf of the four and immediately challenged Cotton to a £1,000 singles. The British player would have none of it, just as in 1975 Nicklaus refused an immense offer to play Miller. Probably the thinking of both of them was the same: if, let us say, you fail to win a particular stroke-play event little harm is done to your reputation, but there is no doubt at all that to lose a match over the very fair length of 72 holes creates a strong impression that the other man is the better. Nicklaus now, and Cotton then, were reckoned the best around and did not want to forfeit the kudos whether for £1,000 or the fabulous figure offered for a Nicklaus versus Miller match.

Locke had to content himself with playing and beating the Open champion Reg Whitcombe, an achievement repeated against Dick Burton in 1939.

The ten-stone stripling then went to war and became a highly-competent pilot on Liberators, flying 100 missions in the Mediterranean theatre. For two and a half years he did not touch a golf club and at the end of the war emerged as the 14-stone heavyweight who was often taken to be more than 40 years old before he reached 30.

In 1946 he campaigned in Britain and took the Harry Vardon trophy, which is awarded for the best tournament stroke average. Perhaps his sweetest moment was to walk to the 1st tee at Hoylake in the semi-final of the matchplay Championship for a match with . . . Henry Cotton. But Cotton, though approaching 40, had a few shots left in his locker and took the match after a close contest.

His next matchplay encounter went altogether differently. Sam Snead was brought over to South Africa to play a series against Bobby. Snead won twice, Locke won 12 times and there were a couple of halves that Sam was no doubt relieved to get. He later commented that Bobby never asked where the pins were: if he could get the ball on the green, the putt was sure to go in.

Walter Hagen was a great believer in the theory that, to prove himself a Master, an American golfer must take the British Open. Amongst others, he persuaded Ben Hogan to come over in 1953 to Carnoustie. In the 1930s, he had played with Locke in South Africa and had put this point of view in reverse: Locke should attempt to prove himself in America. Encouraged by his success against Snead, at the time, with Hogan, Demaret and Nelson at the top of the US golf tree, Locke duly arrived in the spring to play in the Masters. His swing was duly analyzed on the practice ground and opinions were unfavourable. It was too long (Bobby swung a club considerably past the horizontal), lacked power and there was also a weak grip with the left hand and, worse, 'the guy duck-hooked all his shots!'.

Locke started his campaign steadily but did not threaten to win, finishing in tenth place on the Augusta course, which in fact is said to favour anyone who draws his shots. He next competed in the Carolina's Open and won it. On to Houston, and another cheque for first place. At Fort Worth, Texas, alas, 'only' third place but there followed a dramatic encounter in the *Philadelphia Inquirer* Open Tournament with the great Hogan. Ben led after two rounds by five strokes after starting 65, 69. Locke picked up seven strokes on him in the third round to go into the last two ahead, and in the end won comfortably.

This, perhaps, was the win that made Bobby a name in America. There was wonder that a 'guy from the jungle' could have beaten Hogan after allowing him a lot more than a headstart. By now, the Americans were beginning to think that there must be something right with Bobby's swing after all. The knowledgeable were beginning to see that, for example, Locke was a very good driver indeed. The ball might not go boring into the far distance but it did go far enough and it was nearly always on the fairway. Then a few minutes later Locke was able to take hold of his putter with the rusty iron head and hickory shaft, take a couple of measured practice putts and then move it on and down.

The next tournament, a round robin of 16 players, again resulted in a first-place cheque. Only third next time out and on to the US Open. Locke had to keep to level par over the last nine holes to tie Snead and Lew Worsham, and he did not quite – third again. For a change of scene he moved off to Canada for the Canadian Open where a score of 268 made him a comfortable winner, the first British player, said Locke, to win since 1914. Though a native South African, Locke tended to refer to himself as 'British' and seemed to feel that when he won in America it was a triumph not for South African golf alone but for the British Empire. *Sic transit gloria mundi.*

By this time, Locke had become *the* name on the US circuit. Accordingly George S. May, promoter of the Tam O'Shanter Tournament in Chicago, offered him $5,000 appearance money. Locke went. This was big money at the time, for a dollar really was a dollar. He justified his price in the first round by going round in 66, and came somewhere near maintaining this form for the rest of the Tournament. He reached the 14th tee needing to play the last five holes in two over par to win. He three-putted that one and then dropped another shot on the next. In the end it was a playoff for $7,000, at that time easily the biggest prize in golf. Ed Oliver covered the 36 holes in 146, which was fair; good enough to finish six strokes behind Bobby.

He played in two more tournaments thereafter, finishing first and second, and was in second place for winnings, a handful of dollars behind Jimmy Demaret, who had played the whole season on the tour rather than, as Locke, from April only.

One of the things most remembered about Bobby Locke today is that he competed in America and did very well. I do not think it is realized just how good that performance was, only rivalled by Byron Nelson, who suddenly found out all the secrets of how to play golf in 1944 and won monotonously for a couple of years before breathing a sigh of relief and retiring. But consider Locke's record. Seven tournament wins from a man who had never before played in the US, and in addition a very respectable total of second and third places.

In the years that followed Locke returned to America several times and did very well, though he did not dominate to quite the same extent as in 1947. Perhaps he felt he had proved himself in the hardest school of all and in the future preferred, I think, to play in Britain where, in a sense his career had hardly begun. There was, for instance, the matter of three British Opens in four years still to be won and then a final one in 1957, when people thought Bobby's great days were over.

Most tend to reckon golfing greatness in terms of major championships won. I suspect Bobby Locke did not have this attitude and to a considerable extent thereafter competed in the quieter pastures of Britain where only one of the four major championships is to be won. But his triumphal progress around the US circuit in 1947 has, in its inexorable consistency, been rivalled only by Byron Nelson. There is no one else in sight.

Golden Boy's streak

On 10 July 1976 Johnny Miller, as related elsewhere, won the British Open Championship and for all time established himself as one of the major golfers of this century. For the general run of mankind his greatness had not been in doubt because for several years he had been more written and talked about than any golfer other than Jack Nicklaus.

But for sterner judges there remained the fact that he had won but a single major championship out of the big four: the British and US Opens, the US PGA and the Masters. That victory at

Oakmont in the US Open, seized by a spasm of perfection for a final round of 63 also failed to satisfy many of the cognoscenti. They felt that when Miller went out on that last round he knew he had no logical hope of winning. He had begun with two solid enough rounds and then collapsed to a 76 – and you don't win an Open on a course playing relatively easily with that kind of burden around your neck. Nevertheless, almost before he knew it, Miller found himself in the lead after starting off six strokes behind the leaders. So, those stern judges felt, he had not borne the pressures of going out knowing that you should or may win. They felt that the last round was one of those that many players have produced when there is no longer anything to lose. Even that it was a great round of golf was denied, because Oakmont was not the course of lightning greens that it almost invariably is through the years. It had rained and rained and rained. Any shot that hit the green stuck and Miller's shots were hitting and sticking near the flags. For the putts that then followed a golfer didn't need the nerve and delicacy Oakmont normally required: in other words you could send your ball firmly at the hole knowing that there was no danger of its gliding past and then on and on. But no one else remotely approached Miller's scoring.

Undoubtedly the title helped Miller. He felt that he had proved himself even if not everyone agreed and from the beginning of 1974 to about the same time the following year he plundered tournaments to a degree rivalled only by Byron Nelson 30 years before, the stripling Horton Smith in 1928 and Bobby Locke.

In this phase his golf far outdistanced the stuff anyone else was playing, with the exception of Jack Nicklaus, who was having quite a year himself.

Miller began by winning a tournament played over three Californian courses – Pebble Beach, Spyglass Hill and Cyprus Point – and stood four strokes in the lead after three rounds had been played. Bad weather meant that the final round had to be abandoned. Then on to the Phoenix Open, where Miller played four consecutive rounds under the par of 71: 69, 69, 66, 67. This Tournament was, however, not the triumphal procession that many of Miller's later victories were to be. He did not lead until the end of the third round and then it was a lead shared with Miller Barber, owner of just about the most unorthodox swing in top-class golf.

Barber takes the club back very much on the outside and then loops it around until he eventually comes into the hitting area along an entirely normal path. But Barber's swing is, even so, far closer to the norm than that employed by the great Irishman James Bruen. Bruen did not merely take the club back on the outside: he lifted it away from his body and then looped it around before lashing the clubhead at the ball as if he were using a whip. The results here were varied: enormous length from the tee, great powers of recovery from the rough which he often visited, a fair number of clubs that broke just below the grip because they could not take the stress and, finally, damage to a wrist that put Bruen out of competitive golf.

By the time he reached the 14th tee Johnny Miller was five ahead of the field but put his drive behind a tree, bunkered his second shot and then three-putted. Meanwhile the equally mercurial Lanny Wadkins was having a very good day. After the 16th he had caught Miller but dropped a shot on the 17th, while Miller birdied. It was now all on the last and Wadkins did not falter. He hit two driver shots into the green and then holed the long putt for an eagle. Miller, behind, had to get another birdie to win. He did so and that was two wins in a row and a new aim – to be the first man since Arnold Palmer to win three tournaments consecutively. On to Tucson. For the first round he took only 25 putts and, as the rest of his game was functioning almost equally well, that meant a 62, over a course measuring 7,300 yards. Johnny kept the momentum going the next day and at one point in his round was 14 under par for the Tournament. He then faltered a little and finished in 71 but was still good enough to give him a lead of four strokes. He had the same score in the next round though again his outward half of 32 had promised a lot better. Miller completed the formalities the following day and then took a week off.

For the Hawaian Open Jack Nicklaus put in his second appearance of the season, determined not to yield his position as number one on the US circuit. He began 65, 67, nine shots better than

Miller, and the Tournament was almost over after two days. Nevertheless Miller's four rounds of 71, 70, 70, 70 meant that he had played 15 consecutive rounds under par.

The Bob Hope Desert Classic followed and again Miller finished well behind the winner, Bert Yancey, who had included a 61 amongst his rounds. But Miller played five rounds under par and the consecutive streak now stood at 20.

The Riviera Club at Los Angeles saw the end of Miller's run when, although he finished fifth, he had a 73 in the last round. In the next tournament he finished well down the field and decided that enough was enough for the time being. He returned to the tour for the Sea Pines Heritage Classic, saying he felt restored to health and vigour. Opening rounds of 67, 67 gave him a lead of six strokes and he cruised to an eventual comfortable victory by three strokes on one of the tightest courses on the tour. His next victory came in the Tournament of Champions, for which the field consists of 25 players who have won in the previous year. Miller began with an unpromising 75 but improved to 69, 67, 69 for a victory by one stroke, his fifth in 11 entries that year.

For the rest of the season his appearances were spasmodic and he performed relatively poorly in the major championships. By the time he competed in the Westchester Classic he had been off the tour for two months. He opened with 69, 68 and at that point was four behind the leader. So Miller improved to a 65, one of his best rounds of the season. Of course the actual score tells us little about how good a round has been played, although 'how many' not 'how' is what counts when the cheques and trophies are being handed out. Nevertheless most of us feel that putting and chipping should not count for as much as they do. We feel that the great round of golf consists of a stream of shots flowing up the middle of the fairway, followed by a succession of crisp iron shots of even more precision. Thereafter the putting should be competent. In this sense, Bobby Jones's 66 at Sunningdale while qualifying for the 1926 British Open seized the imagination at the time because he holed only one putt of any length. For the rest, his score was achieved by hitting all the greens in one or two shots with no miserable scrabbling of the ball towards the hole from off the putting surface.

By this standard, Miller's round in the Westchester was perhaps better. He hit *every* green in one or two strokes and was off the fairway only once. Contrast this with a round of 72 the author once played when he hit not a single good tee shot but did at least manage to get the iron shots somewhere near the greens and occasionally even *on* them. But what chipping and putting then ensued . . .

Miller went round the next day in 67; that was another victory and also meant that he had won $250,000 for the year.

In the World Open there was a running confrontation with Jack Nicklaus. Miller began with 73 but then had a 63 which gave him the lead. After three rounds they were level on 209 and then, paired, both played the final 18 in 72. There was a four-way playoff with Bob Murphy and Frank Beard. Murphy dropped out on the first playoff hole and then the three remaining reached a par five in two apiece, with Miller being only 12 feet from the hole. Beard and Nicklaus three-putted. Miller didn't.

His final win on the US circuit was in the Kaiser International which he won by the overwhelming margin of eight shots from Lee Trevino and Billy Casper. Such dominance is indeed a keynote of Miller's play. When the mood is with him he always aims to make a substantial lead overwhelming, where others begin to play defensively and try to avoid dropping shots rather than go for birdies. But Miller attacks to the end as shown, for example, by the fact that he made far more use of his driver from the tee *after* he had built a formidable lead over Severiano Ballesteros in the last round of the 1976 British Open.

There was one more overwhelming victory to come in 1974 at the tail end of the year. This time it was in Japan, where he took the Dunlop Phoenix in December. Rounds of 69, 69, 69, 67 gave him a total of 274, seven strokes ahead of the second-place finisher. During the course of the Tournament, he also had to contend with a change of clubs. All golfers know that feeling of expectation aroused when there is a gleaming new set of irons clinking in the bag. In their unblemished state they look to have the precision of surgical instruments but very soon we find ourselves having to make remarks about how we 'haven't got used to these new irons yet'. For the top professional moving from country to country there is a different problem. He may be contracted to use Mac-Gregors in the US, Slazenger in the UK, Dunlop in Australia – and so on. As Mark McCormack relates in his *World of Professional Golf 1974* Miller was contracted to use Japanese clubs. But they weren't ready. Never mind, he used one set for his first round and then switched when the contractual set eventually arrived. Perhaps the extent of this achievement can be exaggerated too much. A good golfer should be able to play with just about anything or so 'they' say. This was best illustrated by the story of how Sam Snead once carved himself a driver (shaft and all) out of swamp maple, added to this his trusty wedge and putter and went round his home course in not much worse than par.

But the fact is, although the golfing public believe the emblazoned bags when they tell us that golfer X is playing with manufacturer Y's clubs, this is often not so in the strictest sense. Most have a driver from which they will not be parted, perhaps a fairway wood or a 1 iron, and almost invariably a pitching and sand wedge that they trust. Amongst the favoured clubs have been Snead's driver, Nicklaus's 3 wood and Gary Player's sand wedges.

So if we buy a set of Arnold Palmer, Jack Nicklaus or whoever's autographed clubs, it is probably just the name we get. The player himself has to use them in (let us say) Britain before another lot in South Africa, because he is being very highly paid to do so. But he'd be far happier if he could use the weapons he would choose for himself. Not a few players in fact are renowned for the ways in which they alter what the manufacturer has provided for them. Nicklaus, for example, likes to play with thick grips so that the fingers on his left hand do not meet as he grasps the club; Palmer spends hours in the workshop of his Latrobe home taking off a sliver of metal here, adding a strip of lead tape there, thrusting irons into a vice and adjusting loft and lie.

And what of the players who, though good, haven't a name worth paying for? I once looked in the bag of a man who later reached the top 20 and saw a bewildering mixture: a nameless driver that looked to date from the time when they used to paint steel shafts to make them resemble hickory, a new 3 wood, manufacturer X's long irons, Y's mid irons and Z's pitching clubs . . .

But back to Miller, who was obviously experiencing little difficulty with his myriad sets of clubs.

The year of 1974 was over. On 9 January 1975 Miller was at Phoenix, Arizona. He began with a 67, which was enough to give him the joint lead with two or three other players. But by the end of the second round the second player was no less than six strokes behind. Miller had begun with an eagle and did not go over par during his round. He also had eight birdies and a total of 61.

There have been lower rounds of golf. Gary Player, for instance, had a 59 in the 1974 Brazil Open but this was on a course that measured 6,185 yards against the 6,700 of Phoenix Country Club and had a par of 69 against 71. Several players recorded scores of 60 on the US tournament circuit in the 1950s but this was a period when courses were 'set up' to produce low scores. Sometimes the ladies' tees were used and preferred lies allowed. No doubt at all then that Miller's round was better than any of these until eclipsed by Al Geiberger's 59 in 1977. The Tournament itself was as good as over. Rarely does a top player let a commanding lead slip – Miller did not relax but rather increased his lead. It was a 68 in the third round and then a final 64 for a total of 260, 24 under par and 14 strokes better than Jerry Heard in second place. This was the lowest tournament score for 20 years.

Miller collected his $30,000 and moved to Tucson. On a more formidable course 500 yards longer than Phoenix with a par of 72, he began with a 66, then followed up with 69, 67. After this warm up he played what he described as 'the greatest round of my life'. Again, it was a 61 and gave him a winning score of 263. This time he was 'only' nine strokes ahead of the second-place man, John Mahaffey.

During that final round Miller claimed he'd hit every green and missed only one fairway. Furthermore, every iron shot settled fairly close to the flag so that he was putting for a birdie and the occasional eagle on every hole. He got one eagle and nine birdies. Miller's play was beginning to make a par seem a shot dropped and in fact he was playing with such fire, flair and confidence that this was how it did feel to him. He was wondering about scoring in the 50s and came close to doing so in that last Tucson round: he missed two putts of about a couple of yards and there were two more of the kind of length Miller had come to expect to get into the hole.

Miller's putting had of course been central to this spate of low scoring. You can't be nearly 50 under par for eight rounds unless the hole is looking a favourable size and Miller was remorseless in sinking the ones under a couple of yards that are vital to even adequate scoring. But for the rest of it, his achievements were not at all based on holing putts from unlikely distances – though of course the occasional one did go in. No, he was hitting the ball so well through the green that good scores were bound to follow. As Johnny Miller himself said : 'Happiness is when even your worst shots are still quite good.'

Where could he go from here ? Well Miller didn't manage to do a Byron Nelson and compile an endless succession of tournament victories but then this is surely impossible in the present state of the professional game. The keen edge was dulled a little and though he won again during the season his highest achievements were placing second in the Masters and one behind Tom Watson and Jack Newton, tieing for first place in the 1975 British Open. At the climax of this event Miller demonstrated his 'all or nothing' approach. Bunkered off the 18th fairway and thinking he had to get a birdie to win he took a 6 iron. His ball stayed in the bunker. What followed is to me indicative of Miller's attacking qualities and, perhaps, of the fact that he's not afraid to make a fool of himself. He did not demand a sand wedge of his caddie; he went with the 6 iron again and this time the shot, though off the green, was quite near the flag. To some extent it is remembered that Miller was rash in playing a 6 iron and thereby 'lost' the 1975 Open; to me it's more memorable that he dared to use the thing again.

Speculation about the future is all too liable to be disproved alarmingly quickly. Take the 1976 US Open and the thousands of words written about that. Would Nicklaus do it again ? Just how good was Tom Weiskopf's game at the moment of going to Press and how good or bad was his temperament ? Was Miller depressed or challenged by his loss of form ? So Jerry Pate, barely out of the amateur ranks won it and shortly after took 48 shots on the second nine at Royal Birkdale. Henry Longhurst, reporting midway through the 1974 US Masters, was somewhat premature, for he gave it as his opinion that at long last it could be said that Gary Player was just a little past it, that, like Palmer, he now really was out of the Big Three of world golf. At which point Gary began his move to make himself the undoubted number one for that year.

He won the Masters, romped through the British Open and recorded that 59 in the Brazil Open to round off the season.

So whither Miller? After his win in the 1976 British Open, many were saying that here now was the greatest of them all. Yet this 29-year-old glamour boy of the golf world was already perhaps too old. Nicklaus had won more titles when still under 25, still the fat, crew-cut power house before he heeded his public relations and got the weight down and let the hair grow. No, in terms of major-championship victories, Miller is unlikely to add more than two or three more but these, when added to his unparalleled excellence on the US tournament circuit in 1974 and 1975, should keep the memory green.

Tempo

Every journalist likes to have a peg to hang his story on. Tom Weiskopf supplied a highly-useful one on the final day of of the 1970 US Open. I have heard it about 32 times and I dare say some readers can beat that. The peg? Well, of course, you know already, because it is the first word on this page. Jacklin, leading the field, arrived at the Hazeltine course and opened his locker. Inside was a one-word message from his friend Weiskopf: TEMPO. Tom was reminding Tony that he must keep the poise and rhythm of his swing through the day ahead. Perhaps mental composure was implied as well.

History knows that Tony kept his tempo and won by a formidable margin. Yet Weiskopf's word applied to his own problems far more than to the Tony Jacklin of 1970.

Everyone, including Tom Weiskopf himself, acknowledged that he had an immense talent for the game, was arguably the most naturally-gifted player of them all. His length of drive was exceeded only by a few 'unknowns' on the US circuit who could thrash a golf ball to infinity but did very little else. Weiskopf, on the other hand, had both power and delicacy. If he had a weakness it was that the 'tidying up' areas of his game were less good. Because he missed greens less often than most, his chipping was competent, rather that a dominant feature of his game, but his putting was usually as reliable as the best of them.

Peter Alliss also points out that Tom has a tendency to roll the clubface open on the backswing, the main cause of the occasional extremely wild shot he hits. He also has troubles with his hands as a result of catching baseballs as a youngster.

Yet it was mental tempo and the ability to keep going when the fates seemed ill disposed that Tom appeared to lack most of all. Of course, while these thoughts were being voiced of him, Tom was winning a lot of money. He came to some prominance in 1968, when he won two US events and was third amongst the money winners, and by the end of 1972 had won five. Nevertheless he was by then 30 years old, which used perhaps to be the peak age for a golfer but, in a majority of cases, not any more.

Was he to be one of those great players but . . . who fail to win a major championship? At the time it seemed that Macdonald Smith with a similarly rhythmic, though less-powerful, swing might be his nearest equivalent in golf history though there are others, Leo Diegel, for example, who have almost elbowed their way out of winning an Open. However, most of the great players, sadly though they may have fallen short of potential, in the end manage to pick up a British or US Open somewhere or other along the way.

Like Sam Snead, who won the British Open in 1946 and with a certain lack of *politesse* called it 'just another tournament', Weiskopf had to do it outside his own country. Golf in Britain has suited him well and his image on the British side of the Atlantic is far more attractive than the one he has established on American courses. In the US he is, at least to some extent, thought of as a man in whom boyish charm has been known to give place to a petulant curl of the lip and there are a few golf lockers that have been kicked too hard after not too successful a round. But in Britain, winning or losing, he has yet to put a foot wrong.

But it is better to win than lose and Tom's career can be marked as taking an emphatic turn for the better in the autumn of 1972. The Piccadilly World Match Play was the occasion. In it, the encounter between Tony Jacklin and Lee Trevino – told elsewhere in this book – in retrospect has dominated everybody's memory (except, probably, Tom Weiskopf's). He won the thing quite comfortably. Out went Graham by three and two in the first round and Oosterhuis in the second and on the final day there was

Trevino, overcome by memories of the previous day's drama. Four and three to Tom and a first major championship. Or was it? No doubt at all that the Piccadilly was a very attractive event; similarly there's no doubt either that a mere eight players can never constitute a major championship of any kind unless one precondition is met: the field must include the holders of the US Open, the Masters, the US PGA, the Open . . . well from now on there is room for individual opinion. No need probably from this point on to concentrate on winners of anybody else's open. Perhaps the best British player of the year to add nationalistic spice and certainly an American who has won a formidable amount of money during the year should be automatic invitations. From that point on, the organizers can keep looking at the US if they prefer but it would probably be as well to look as hard at South Africa, Australia and the Far East. After you had done all that, you still might not have a major championship, for no one who has won just three matches can claim to be world matchplay champion.

But when Tom went back to America he certainly felt he had won something worth more than a run-of-the-mill tournament and had glowed under the admiration of the Wentworth golf galleries.

Then early the following year Tom's father died and that made Tom reassess his life in golf. Here was a man as gifted as any in the game's history with a spasmodic record of achievement. He resolved to work harder and, among other things, stop dropping off the US circuit to indulge his delight in hunting trips.

The medicine did not work overnight, however. In April, for instance, he gave one of his worst performances to that date in the US Masters, finishing on 297 but at the Colonial National Invitational he put together a sequence which he called 'the best four rounds I've played'. His 276 gave him victory by a single stroke over Jerry Heard and that Australian, who seldom ventures outside America, Bruce Crampton. Perhaps luck had also turned for Weiskopf. Crampton had come to the last needing 'only' a four to win, drove into rough country, where he buckled the shaft of his sand wedge en route to taking six.

In the Kemper Open, however, Weiskopf did even better. Starting with a 65, during which he missed but a single green, Tom followed with 70, 68, 68 for the low total of 271 and victory by three shots over Lanny Wadkins. No one else was any nearer than six behind. Then in the Philadelphia Classic he won by four clear shots and at the end of it had played 17 consecutive tournament rounds without once exceeding par for the course. In a month he had won a fortune of well over $100,000 even having missed one event while doing a week's training with the National Guard.

Of course he was a favourite for the US Open and justified that status. Alas for Tom, this was the year that Johnny Miller did the impossible by going round Oakmont in 63. The Championship had seemed to be going to one out of Boros, Heard, Palmer, Schlee or Weiskopf and of these Tom was considered to have the best chance. He was the man in form and went out on the last round with a total of 211, against Miller's 216. But, playing an hour ahead, Miller had nine birdies and as the end approached Tom found that he needed too many birdies on the last few holes. He finished in 70 for third place and that was another major championship Tom had not won.

And so to Troon and the British Open (sorry, it is of course simply *the* Open, a harmless-enough chauvinism but one that sometimes leads to a little confusion). The last time Troon had been the venue there had been a memorable win. Palmer had totalled the record 276 that had left all but the gallant Kel Nagle far, far behind.

Weiskopf allowed himself plenty of time to prepare and had eight practice rounds. Nevertheless he was unhappy about his standard of play, feeling unsure how to play certain shots with the 1.62-inch British ball. Jacklin talked technique and matters improved. The course also set special problems, ones that affected not only Tom. An American golfer is accustomed to getting a perfect result from a perfect shot. If a ball goes booming straight down a fairway it should stay on it and when that player arrives at his ball for the next shot he expects a good lie and a reasonably even stance. Not so at Troon. The fairways undulate, abound in hollows, and at times the surface has a crumpled appearance. So a splendid drive may dart off sideways into the rough, or, if it remains on the fairway, a player is still left with a problem such as 'can I get the ball up quickly enough with my 3 wood and out of this hollow?'. And the greatest golfer is no more joyous about sidehill and downhill stances than the club player. He knows he can make the necessary adjustments well enough but he'd far rather not have to.

Bobby Locke always used to say that Troon's greens were the best in the world, a biassed viewpoint perhaps – he won there in 1950 – but whatever the perfection of the surfaces, the greens are both small and narrow. When they are hard the approach shot can bound off unkindly though Palmer at his greatest had shown that a well-struck shot was usually rewarded.

As the days of practice went by the usual man – Jack Nicklaus – was favoured to win but there was a lot of money on Trevino. He had shown good recent form in finishing fourth in the US Open and had won the British the previous two years. Many indeed, after his startling chipping and putting performance in the 1972 Open, felt Lee might attempt the even more unusual this year – walk on the water perhaps? In the event Trevino proved less than divine and was never in contention. Much interest at this stage centred, of course, on Johnny Miller – a 63 in the last round of an Open to win is as supernatural a golfing achievement as the mind can imagine. Tom Weiskopf was also fancied, mainly because he had been at such a peak of form for two months and more, but there were doubts that his game was suited to Troon, especially if there was wind.

Many Opens are lost over the first few holes. A bad start at any level can make a golfer feel that it's just not his week or that he's given too much away to be able to make it up. But this does not apply to Nicklaus, incontestably the greatest player of a last round when there's virtually no hope left. I'm sure he feels he ought to win everything he enters and devotes himself in the earlier rounds to defence – making sure he does not do anything too silly and thus put himself out of the running. Watch him on the last day when he's four or five behind the leader and decides to go for everything . . .

Tom's start must have put bounce into his strides. After missing a birdie putt of about a yard on the 362-yard 1st he birdied three of the next four holes and reached the turn in 33. So far there had been but one error through the green. Tom overshot the 8th with his tee shot but chipped back well and holed the putt. But it was someone else's play on this 126-yard hole that caused more stir than Weiskopf's golf that first day. Gene Sarazen, winner of the British Open in 1932 and of the US in 1922 and 1932, had at the age of 71 decided this was his farewell appearance in a British Open – or indeed any tournament. At the Postage Stamp the TV cameras were watching as he punched in a little 5 iron. The ball went into the hole. The following day Sarazen produced a performance no less startling. This time he bunkered his tee shot beside the green and then sand wedged it directly into the hole. How often, I wonder, has anyone played a hole consecutively without using a putter? Palmer would have liked to be touched by Sarazen's knack on this hole. On the second day like Sarazen he bunkered his tee shot and after much to-ing and fro-ing there was a seven to be written down on the card. Exit Arnold Palmer from the field of former glories.

For Weiskopf there was now the more difficult inward half to play. All day many competitors had scored well going out but less confidently on the return into a 20-mile-an-hour breeze. Not a few cards showed scores in the low 30s for the first half but nearer 40 for the second. Weiskopf and Miller had 35 coming back and this was the best of the day. Tom, playing late, had benefited from a drop in wind speed but had hardly been spurred on by the achievements of his playing partners, Oosterhuis and Tommy Aaron. Both put themselves out of contention in this round. Tom was the only player during the day to birdie the 468-yard 13th, which few indeed reached in two shots. He played a 1 iron that held its line all the way and holed a putt of about five yards. His only serious error came at the last, where he hooked into the rough and went over par.

In the lead, Tom decided on the second day to concentrate on safety, to avoid going over par rather than attempt to make birdies. This time he was out early when the greens were wetter and this seemed to do him no harm at all. Thirty putts were not a bad total. But he by no means did it all on the greens. His driving to the narrow fairways was perfect and he birdied each of the long holes and also the 381 yard 3rd and the 389-yard 7th. The end result was a 67 and, not surprisingly, Tom once more held the lead at the close of play on 135. His closest rivals at this point were Johnny Miller, 138, Bert Yancey at 139 and Jack Nicklaus a shot further off.

Weiskopf's confident advance to victory faltered drastically in the third round, which he played with Miller. On the first hole of all he fluffed a chip and then immediately drove into a bunker. On the 3rd he had a bogey and Miller was level with him at seven under par for the Championship. It is often said that Tom led at Troon from start to finish and this is true insofar as the leader board at the end of the day is concerned, but both leader boards and TV have now conditioned galleries and audiences to think in terms of how many under par X or Y is during the course of a round. So after those few holes Tom was certainly not the Championship leader. Miller was indeed on the attack. He had consecutive birdies from the 6th to the 8th but Tom, fighting back, had nearly matched him by having birdies at two of them. Their play on the Postage Stamp was crucial. Miller had the honour and sent his ball only a little more than a yard from the hole. He could be forgiven glancing at Weiskopf to see if he was hurt! If Tom was, his reaction did not betray it. His ball finished the merest touch closer to the hole and it was now Miller's turn to show resilience, in this Open Championship which was rapidly becoming a match between the pair of them. He holed the putt and the burden was back on Weiskopf's shoulders. He too sank the birdie putt.

Miller still had the honour on the 427-yard 9th and drove long and straight. Weiskopf too drove long but his ball hooked away into the gorse and when he got to it the lie was unplayable, even for his resources of power. If you happen on a golf course to find yourself in a sea of gorse there is little point in picking your ball from one clump of the stuff and then, under a one-stroke penalty, to drop it into another. Weiskopf surveyed the scene. Friendlier territory lay back towards the tee. He walked back about a hundred yards and dropped. Two more strokes, and he was on the green; two putts and that was a six. But Miller had a four to be out in 32 to Weiskopf's 37. The leader boards showed Miller now two strokes better than Weiskopf and Bert Yancey one better. So much for Tom having led this 1973 Open throughout.

The rain was heavy, the rough clinging, but the greens were soft and holding. Both Miller and Weiskopf could rifle in their shots at the flag rather than trust to the pitch and run. Though Troon was now offering target golf, the pin positions were severe – set close to bunkers or in other positions where the player has to dare if he is to finish close by the hole. Weiskopf's passage back to the club-house was not easy – three times he was bunkered – but neverthe-less he was back through the wind and rain in 34 to Miller's 37 and at the day's end was once again the Championship leader.

This is how those who were to feature on the last day stood at that time:

206	Weiskopf	68, 67, 71
207	Miller	70, 68, 69
211	Yancey	69, 69, 73
213	Coles	71, 72, 70
215	Nicklaus	69, 70, 76

There were obviously only two men in it unless one of Yancey, Coles and Nicklaus could repeat the kind of scoring that Johnny Miller had produced in the recent US Open. Two of them did, or nearly so. Neil Coles had performed steadily through the Cham-pionship and in the last round he did considerably better than that. At the end he was signing a card for a 66 and he had set the target of 279 that both Miller and Weiskopf would have to beat. Towards the end of the Championship there was just a chance that the unflamboyant Coles would find himself edging forward into the limelight, if the leaders were crippled by fears of winning. Jack Nicklaus too had a very good day, equalling his lowest round in any US or British Open with a 65. All hope gone, barring miracles or collapse, Jack banished thoughts of his 76 the day before and this time round took 11 shots less.

In an atmosphere reminiscent of a playoff, the leaders duly posed for photographs on the 1st tee and then set out into the heavy rain. Miller immediately went over par on the 1st and found himself three behind Tom after three holes played. He held this position to the turn, which he reached in 34, while Miller took two shots more.

The 481-yard 11th, the Railway Hole, is perhaps Troon's most fearsome. You drive over about 200 yards of rough and from that point are menaced by the out-of-bounds railway all the way up to and including the greenside. In 1962, Palmer's playing of this hole while winning the Open that year, if not legendary, is a part of golf folklore: par, birdie, birdie, and then to round things off, eagle.

Weiskopf and Miller both birdied it. Then a glimmer of light for
Miller on the next. Tom missed the green; Miller had a six-yard
putt for a birdie. But Miller missed and Weiskopf chipped close
by the hole. The gap between them remained three.

At last, on the 468-yard 13th, Miller did improve his position.
Weiskopf hit a poor mid iron and missed the green comfortably.
This time his little pitch shot was not close and Miller parred the
hole to be two behind. The 15th proved crucial. After three shots
Weiskopf lay dead. Miller had a long putt of about eight yards for
his birdie. His bold attempt threatened the hole but in the event
stopped a couple of feet past. Now he had this one to stay only two
behind. He settled into his stance and there came a roar from a
nearby gallery. Coles had sunk a putt to go nine under par for the
Championship. Britain was not going to win but at least there was
something to cheer about. Miller settled to his ball again and missed.
Farewell to the 1973 British Open? The question mark is there
because in golf, and any other sport where tension can play a
major role, you never can tell until the last drive has been hit and
you arrive on the green with five putts to win the Open and are
fairly confident that even God cannot make you putt that badly
. . . can he?

Well Miller had another chance immediately after. Weiskopf
decided to play safe with an iron from the tee on the 542-yard 16th
and was fairly well short after his second. Miller hit a couple of
woods to 20 or 30 yards of the green and then got his little pitch
to a couple of yards. But he missed the putt and the position was
unchanged.

The 17th at Troon is a 223-yard par three of the most testing
kind: you have to be able to hit a long shot straight with enough
bite on your ball for it to hold on a slightly-domed green that
throws off a shot anything less than very well struck. Weiskopf
played first and hit a 3 iron full at the flag; Miller was on, but only
just and grateful to get his three. So, at the last, Tom knew that a
six on this 425-yard hole would be good enough. He hit an iron
from the tee again but still needed to use only a 7 iron for his
approach. To ease his mind a little, Miller then put his approach
into a greenside bunker, an event more heartening by this stage to
Neil Coles than Weiskopf. Miller was suddenly playing for joint

second place and played a superb bunker shot to a couple of feet, holed the putt and that was a tie on 279 with Coles. Tom had four putts for the Open but that is hardly a glorious way to leave the centre of the stage. Weiskopf sent his shot from the fringe of the green to a couple of feet and then holed the putt for a total of 276 and, incidentally, a championship played without three-putting. This is not now a record, but his 276 total was at the time, jointly with Arnold Palmer's score of 11 years earlier.

So Tom Weiskopf had emphatically won his first Open, but the year was by no means over. There were more tournaments and a couple of hundred thousand dollars or so still to be banked, on the way to a recognized total of $349,000 for the year. And of course there were other winnings that do not count in compiling the league table of who has won the most – the US World Series, played off by the winners of the British and US Opens, the Masters and the US PGA, for example.

Earlier came the Canadian Open, an event a little too closely linked to the US circuit in that it attracts relatively few from outside North America. Nevertheless an open championship is always coveted. Peter Alliss's father, Percy, for instance, thought it worthwhile making the laborious three-week journey from his club job in Berlin in order to compete in 1931. He tied for first place on 292 with Walter Hagen. Hagen in the end made the Canadian his last significant open championship but Alliss took him to the 37th hole of the playoff before the deed was done. Weiskopf won far more easily by two clear strokes. He had won five of the last eight events for which he had entered.

At the dying of the golf year comes the World Series of Golf, an attempt to imitate the baseball event of the same name. Weiskopf, Nicklaus, Aaron and Miller were the qualifiers. Weiskopf began by hitting shots in most directions other than the right ones. However, after nine holes Tom got his tempo back again. Following his opening 71, he had a 66 to emerge a very clear winner.

Nineteen seventy-three was most certainly Tom Weiskopf's year, yet at the end of it Nicklaus still had an edge in terms of money won and also a stroke average of 69.8 per round to Tom's 70.2. An heir apparent had certainly become a king but not *the* king.

So matters have remained. Nicklaus the number one, Miller

spasmodically in close pursuit, Gary Player having won two major championships since Weiskopf's British Open while Tom has not added to his score. It may be that the vow to justify his talent was fulfilled by the achievements of 1973 and that Tom may not prove to have the single mindedness to win and keep on winning, to will the chips close and to hole the vital putts of a Player or Nicklaus and, more recently, Tom Watson.

But win or lose, for me he's the golfer that gives the most aesthetic pleasure with that swing that coils back slowly, almost gently, and begins its path back to the ball without urgent acceleration. The pace is there by the time the ball is met. Power with poise, and even a certain elegance.

The impregnable achievement

In 1930 R T Jones Junior, 'Bob' to his friends and 'Bobby' to admirers and the public at large, accomplished what came to be called the 'Grand Slam' or, a little more grandiloquently, the 'Impregnable Quadrilateral'. As we all know, but just possibly one or two of you don't, this consisted of, first, the winning of the British Amateur, then the British Open and then the US Open before – for Jones the easiest of the lot – the US Amateur.

This is a feat that no one, even the most improbable of supermen with two bionic arms and computerized thought processes is at all likely to repeat. For a start, the man has to be an *amateur*. Only one man since Jones's day has had the equipment and early maturity even to allow his thoughts to dwell, however briefly, on the notion. That man, of course, is Jack Nicklaus. But Nicklaus belongs to an era in which the pickings for professionals are so high as to be irresistible in their attractions. As a well-known amateur golfer it is possible to earn a very nice living indeed selling, for example, insurance, or beer, but a leading amateur comes close to earning a life fortune, immediately he turns professional, for endorsing slacks, socks, and a multitude of other products that are only on the periphery of golf. So Nicklaus duly turned professional and, having come very close indeed to winning the US Open as an amateur in 1960 (Palmer's first and only win, Hogan's last sustained attempt) it was not long before he had proved that he might well True, there was a great deal of talk after the event about how Ray have been the man to take over the grand-slamming mantle of the great Jones: by the end of 1963 he had won the US Open, the Masters and the US PGA. But not all in the same year, of course, and it was also a few more years before he took the British Open. Despite Nicklaus's unparalleled achievements as both tournament and major-championship winner, it is an undeniable fact that only Ben Hogan has produced a feat as a professional in one year at a similar level to Jones's: the winning of the US Masters, US Open and British Open in 1953.

Possibly there is one other considerable amateur that might have rivalled Jones. He is a relative newcomer and surprisingly has not been devoted the attention so far that has, for example, poured down upon Ben Crenshaw, for one and Tom Watson for another. I am talking about Jerry Pate. There he was in Britain in 1975 performing with little distinction in a victorious US Walker Cup team and a year later he was US Open champion having played one of the most perfect iron shots ever seen in the moment of truth to the side of the last hole in Atlanta.

And on to Royal Birkdale, as related elsewhere, and in due course a round of 86 . . . Never mind, neither Jones nor Nicklaus has won the Canadian Open (not that Jones competed, to my knowledge). Jerry Pate has. He recorded rounds of 69, 67, 68 and then sharpened up his game for a last round in 63.

Today then, we must think in terms that Jones's feat is no longer possible: a man would have to play too impossibly well for selected stretches of time over about five months.

Yet this is exactly what Jones did *not* do. He later felt that he had played reasonably well in each of his major championship victories during 1930 and had perhaps played more consistently than before. Yet there were no thoughts in retrospect that his golf had been at a consistently superlative level. But in his day Jones was good enough to win when not playing in top form. Although today Nicklaus is the automatic favourite in any championship he enters he is really not expected to win – merely to have the best chance amongst a mass of players who might suddenly reach to the peaks during any particular week. Think, for instance, of Ray Floyd. Who, including Ray himself, would have expected such dominance of the 1976 US Master's field from almost the first stroke played?

had decided to put a 5 wood in the bag and throw out the accustomed 1 iron just for the one tournament. Writers are always seeking the elusive reason why a golfer played so well one week as opposed to another and the winning golfer will give him one: he decided to put a 5 wood in the bag, found this old putter in an attic, decided to go for the flag every time – and so on.

But when Jones competed in the days of his mature greatness the question was whether or not anyone could beat him. Consider the man's record in the British and US Opens. Jones won the US Open four times out of eight attempts from 1923 to 1930. He won the British Open three times between 1926 and 1930 and the latter is the achievement most worthy of legend: he competed only three times in that period. Whereas Jack Nicklaus has won the British Open twice and played in it about 15 times. And what of the other legendary figure of Jones's day, Walter Hagen? Well the truth of it is that the incomparable Walter failed even once to win the US Open after Jones arrived on the scene but won the British four times, all victories achieved while Bobby Jones was safely at home in Atlanta, Georgia. This may seem to belittle the achievements of Hagen. The point I wish to make is simply this: no one ever asked if Bobby could hold off the Hagen, Sarazen, Horton Smith or whoever challenge; they speculated about whether any one of these might be able, over four championship rounds, to stop Jones. As a generalization, the answer was that, no, they could not.

The year of the Grand Slam both began and ended with Jones completely dominant. In between, he had feet of clay. He had but one unfulfilled ambition left: to win the British Amateur. Though he had not competed in it often, it did rankle that he had failed to win it. Gary Player has spoken much of the fact that he has won each of the major titles twice, thus making a sort of double Grand Slam (not of course in anything like the same years) and Jones felt that, never mind how many US Open and Amateur titles he had, and whatever the total might eventually be for British Open victories, there really was a most deplorable gap in his personal record book for the British Amateur. Today it is difficult to see why this was so significant to Jones. Now a US Amateur title is merely prelude to greater events upon the broader professional stage and the majority of British players of quality turn professional before they have given themselves more than a shot or two at the Amateur. Of course, there have been a few – Joe Carr and Michael Bonallack are notable examples – who have won it a few times, but they have threatened only remotely to win a professional tournament of any kind. But Jones was worried about it, felt that his record was incomplete until his name was on the British Amateur Championship cup.

For once he abandoned his regime of playing friendly four-balls and competing only in the championships, and opened his 1930 season unusually early.

He began by getting himself beaten by the new comet on the US scene, Horton Smith. Jones first had a 67, followed with a 75 and then a 65. This put him level with Horton at 207. After four rounds Jones was a shot worse and that meant second place.

He next entered the South-Eastern Open at Augusta. This was not, of course, at Augusta National, which Jones himself helped to design in the early 1930s, and followed by initiating the US Masters in 1934. Both course and the Tournament are Jones's finest memorials. The course is enjoyable for the duffer and a severe test of the best, particularly on account of the speed and subtlety of its greens. And the Tournament, which began from Jones's notion that it would be a pleasant idea to invite a variety of leading golfers, whom in nearly every case he knew well, to play Augusta when it was looking its best in the spring, has after 40 years or so become the greatest tournament in the world. A matter of opinion? – certainly, but the Masters has one advantage over the other major championships: it is played on the same course each year.

In the South-Eastern Open, Jones spreadeagled the field. After a steady first two rounds, he recorded a 69 and then played the first 11 holes of his final round in 37 strokes, which meant he had only to par the last few holes for a winning margin nearing 20. Although so vast a lead caused Jones to lose concentration from this point on, he still won the Tournament in as convincing a style as has ever been achieved.

Nineteen thirty was a year when the Walker Cup, which had yet to be won by Britain, was due to be held at Royal St George's, Sandwich. This then was Jones's first engagement for the British season and after the cup had duly been retained by a margin even

more humiliating for British golf than usual Jones was set for what
he felt might be his final attempt at the British Amateur Championship on the course that he revered above all others, St Andrews.
Golfers who play there but once, tend to leave wondering what all
the fuss is about, for St Andrews (unlike, for example, Turnberry
or Muirfield) does not reveal its quality or challenge at first sight.
I personally have never heard anyone speak well of it who has
played it just once, while for Turnberry, Wentworth, Birkdale,
Muirfield and the few other great British courses, recognition of
the test they set is almost immediate.

Bobby Jones was above all a gentleman and he had kept his
mouth commendably shut on the subject of St Andrews after a
disastrous encounter with it in 1923, but renewed acquaintance
with it in 1927 when winning the Open there had dispatched all
the sour thoughts. If he were to set the seal on his career by getting
his name on the British Amateur cup there was nowhere at all he
would rather do it than in the Kingdom of Fife.

But the trouble with the British Amateur, no matter where
played, was that it was a matchplay competition and all the
matches except the final were played over 18 holes. And the greater
the golfer, the less it seems does he love either matchplay or the
short 18-hole contest. It is just so entirely possible that the great
man will be a bit off his game for an hour and the not-at-all great
will have an enchanted hour and send the irons in at all the flags
and hole all the putts. Exit the great one, fighting a gallant rear-
guard action, by something like five and four. This had happened
to Jones on more occasions than he truly cared to remember in both
Britain and America.

But at least the first round should be all right. He was drawn
against a Nottingham golfer, Sid Roper, of whom opinions were not
flattering. It was hardly likely that he would score fewer than five
on anything other than a par three from time to time.

Par on the opening holes at St Andrews was 4, 4, 4, 4, 5. Roper's
scoring was 4, 4, 4, 4, 4. And if any general criticism could be
made of Jones's play over a stretch of 18 holes it would be that he
was apt to start tentatively, pull himself together and play super-
latively from, let us say, the 5th to the 15th and then become a
little careless with a great round within his grasp.

But this time, Jones was not tentative. After those five opening holes he was five under par and four up. This included a little matter of holing a long bunker shot at a par four for a two. Poor Sid, playing almost the game of his life, was virtually out of the hunt in the first half hour.

Jones and Roper continued in much the same vein to the end. But for a stymie at the par-three 8th which cost him a five, Bobby would have reached the turn in 31. At this time, if your opponent's ball in matchplay happened to lie in your path to the hole that was just too bad (later the rules were changed). You had to knock your putt wide of it and send the next one in or take your niblick (a sort of heavyweight 9 iron) and try to pop your ball over his. (Personally I relish playing an informal Sunday morning four-ball under these rules where one can forget about achieving perfection on the green and concentrate on getting in the way of the opposition, but no one will agree to give it a try. We all want to boast in the bar about gross 77s and net 64s.)

But stymie or not, that outward half, and the steady golf that followed, was good enough for Jones to surmount the first hurdle comfortably. He had survived one of those encounters in which his opponent had apparently played far above his normal game but Jones had still won.

Then came the match that St Andrews had been anticipating while the first two rounds were played. In the third round, Jones would meet Cyril Tolley, the holder and – with Roger Wethered – the leading British amateur of his day. Indeed Tolley's day lasted longer than most for he was still a formidable golfer after the Second World War, result of a full-flowing swing and a delicate touch on and around the greens. If anyone could do it, Tolley was undoubtedly the man to stop Jones, his chances increased by the briefer cut and thrust of 18 holes.

As it proved, this was the match of all those he played during his career that Jones remembered the most vividly in later years. The setting was right – St Andrews – and the weather helped also to produce the aura of a fight to the death between the gods as the wind blew at gale force and the greens became increasingly glassy. For all the shots they had to brace themselves against the force of the wind and also use keen judgment about exactly what kinds of shots were needed into, with, or across the wind and of how the

J.H. Taylor, early 1920s

Harry Vardon, 1921

Walter Hagen at Sandwich, 1928

Bobby Jones at Hoylake, 1930

The top of the backswing: Ben Hogan and Peter Alliss

Just after impact: Michael Bonallack and Ben Hogan

The follow-through: Johnny Miller, Tom Watson

The end of the swing: Sam Snead, Gene Littler

ball would behave as it hovered in the air and eventually alighted on green and fairway.

Tolley began with a top from the first tee but this was not a fore-taste of what was to come. As a result he lost the 1st hole to a par but battle was then joined in earnest. If today the scoring looks none too impressive, it must be remembered how testing the conditions were.

Tolley counter attacked immediately by winning the 2nd and then went one up at the 4th. On the 7th Jones squared the match and took the lead on the next before losing the 9th with a five to a three. All square at the turn. So the match continued on the road home, with Jones no less than three times taking a one-up lead and then immediately losing it. All square when they reached the most famous stretch of all at St Andrews, the Road Hole, then a par five. They drove long with Tolley's the longer shot. Jones had to play first and was confronted with the following problem: there was a bunker between him and the flag. Should he attempt to carry it and also risk continuing into the road? Jones decided to play left with the aim of avoiding the bunker but to leave himself an easy enough chip to the flag. His shot was struck perhaps a little too well, pitched level with the bunker and bounded into the crowd – and back again to the edge of the green. Tolley had an open shot at the flag but pitched a little too short and eventually had to play a delicate little lob for his third over the bunker. In the end it was a half in fours.

The controversy continued for years. Had Jones deliberately aimed at the crowd, counting on their forming a near-impenetrable barrier? You may think that if he had it was very sensible of him. To the tournament player of today, if he can stand the pressure of the thousands watching his every twitch and sniff, it is reckoned very useful to have a huge gallery following you round or, more precisely, packing the sides of fairways and the approaches to and backs of greens. As I heard Peter Alliss say in a TV commentary: 'Oops, he's hit someone on the head and, yes, he's been lucky . . . there's his ball now running back into the middle of the fairway.' Let us hope the spectator survived with equal luck!

But the Jones era was a more gentlemanly one and Jones pro-tested that he would never have deliberately aimed at a cluster of spectators, that he had indeed tried to wave them back before attempting his shot.

So Jones and Tolley faced the home hole at St Andrews all square and the Grand Slam, that one American sports writer had predicted in an idle moment when there was nothing much to write about, had yet to get off the ground. With a following wind, both drove close to the 18th green and after their run ups, Jones putted first and missed. So (and history must be grateful to him) did Tolley.

It ended on the next when Jones's putt for a three was dead, inches from the hole, stymieing Tolley who anyway had a longish one for a half.

This match made all that followed possible but it was still only the third round safely past. There were alarms still ahead. In the fifth round for instance, Jones got to four up with five to play but found himself playing the last with his lead cut to a single hole and an eventual putt of a couple of yards to hole. And then in the 7th he was two down with five to go at which point his opponent kindly drove out of bounds . . . At last he was in the final and that would be over the 36 holes that Jones, though modest, felt was a distance over which he could beat anyone.

The opponent was Roger Wethered, who, though he played well, was struggling for a half at nearly every hole. After the morning round it was almost all over and ended in a seven and six win for Jones. The single remaining major championship trophy was at last in his hands.

Well, as he was in Britain anyway, he might as well have another shot at the British Open. And so to Hoylake a couple of weeks later. Jones felt as relaxed as that about the contest. He had completed the work of a decade to win each of the titles that mattered to him and this British Open held little more than the attraction of winning a major title. The same motive, for instance, that draws Jack Nicklaus over to Britain for the Open when he could not be lured to such an event as the Piccadilly World Matchplay or other events where the appearance money would be high, the prize money acceptable and prestige not entirely lacking.

After one round Jones held the joint lead with two golfers of note, Henry Cotton, who had already given many a foretaste of future glory but was to take four more years before fulfilling promise by winning at Sandwich, and Macdonald Smith, the man whom Bing Crosby, with perhaps 50 years of golfing memories, described as having the most flowing and rhythmic swings of them all. Their 70s represented good scoring, even by today's standards, yet Jones's round could have been a very great deal better. He had putted superbly and holed nothing. Again and again the approach putts had coasted up to the hole and he had been left with just a tap in. But a tap in goes down on the card as a stroke used just as much as a lancing iron shot or long, fairway-splitting drive.

After the second round he was where everyone expected him to be : out alone in front after a 72. Fred Robson was just a shot behind and further off were Horton Smith, the new comet, on 145 and then Archie Compston, arguably the best British golfer of the day, on 147. Archie was a man who could score phenomenally well when the mood came. His annihilation of Walter Hagen in a challenge match at Moor Park in April 1928 was relatively recent in the public mind.

Compston's start in the third round at Hoylake is a vivid illustration of how, just occasionally, a golf match or championship can swing utterly in a matter of minutes only. He set off with these figures : 4, 3, 4, 2. Bobby Jones, secure in a lead over Compston at this point of five clear strokes, began : 4, 5, 6, 3. End of clear lead.

Although Compston did not quite keep up his early momentum he nevertheless played one of open championship golf's great rounds up to that point in time. In fact, there was yet another spurt in the round when Archie went 3, 3, 3, 2 from the turn, while Jones was 3, 3, 4, 3 – also excellent scoring. Yet Jones was playing solidly enough, except, perhaps, for that six on the 3rd, for every par five had for Jones a green that he expected to hit in two shots, wind allowing. But he faltered over the final stretch to the club-house, having four fives in the last five holes. Compston had come dazedly in with a 68; Jones later with 74. So the position in the drama was: 215 Compston, 216 Jones.

There were, of course, others by no means yet out of it but as the afternoon round began it seemed that the 1930 British Open was a straight fight between Compston and Jones. This most certainly was not at all how things turned out.

In fact, everyone played a qualifying round on Monday and

Tuesday. Wednesday and Thursday saw the first two rounds played and then came the grand climax on Friday: two full rounds. As regards the British Open, 1965 was the last year that had a 36-hole final day.

Compston had a nightmare round of a sort that shows how, in golf, you do not merely play better (or worse) on one *day* than another. Compston proved that there can be just as much difference between a morning and afternoon's outing. The 68 became an 82. Although an Open player could at the time afford one poorish round and three steady ones, an 82 any time was the end of the affair.

Long behind Compston, Jones played steadily for a while and on the 8th tee needed two fours to be out in 35. He was faced by a par five of 480 yards, the sort that he had no doubt of reaching in two shots. Well Bobby missed the green with his second shot, but by a small margin. His ball was about ten yards from the putting surface at the foot of a downslope. All that had to be done was to knock it up the slope and to somewhere near the pin and that would have been a four or, at worst, a five. Bobby's third shot, alas, was weak and his next only a little stronger. He had a putt of about three yards to hole for the par five. He stroked it firmly but the ball missed and ran a foot past. Irritably he tapped it at the hole – and missed. From nowhere there was a seven to be written down. Well, we've all written the figure seven down on our cards often enough but to take five strokes from just off the green is an experience to remember for you and I as well as the Bobby Joneses of this world. Jones remembered the experience all right. It seems that every blade of grass on that perfidious upslope was etched on his memory but for the moment he was able to put it behind him. He parred the next to turn in what had become a none-too-heroic 38. There followed a sequence of five fours. That sounds good steady stuff but two of the holes were par threes which, although Jones never confesses to it and he'll admit a fault more readily than most, seem to me to have very frequently been his Achilles' Heel. For instance, once upon a time at Sunningdale, while qualifying for the British Open, he played what is still regarded as just about perfection in a round of golf. No absurd putts were holed and all the greens at the par fours and fives were duly struck in two shots.

The only flaw in the gemstone was that, yes, he missed the green at a par three . . .

But this time Jones again managed to dominate Hoylake's intimidating finish where so many finish with a flourish of fives. He had a four at the 14th and missed another by a whisker at the next. The 16th measured 532 yards, which even today is not at all the sort of distance easy to cover in two shots. There came a moment to rival one or two others in Jones's great career and without doubt it was the key instant that won him this Open.

He hit a long drive precisely to the dogleg but then pulled his second shot a trifle. He was bunkered. Could he get down in two more? Easily, it must have seemed. Using a club he had hardly tried out before, Jones flipped his ball to the lip of the hole and tapped it in for a four. (The 14-club rule was not then in force. Although Jones, like Vardon, played usually with a far shorter set than this he, like others, did carry the odd club for special occasions. Walter Hagen, for instance, during this period carried a lefthand club for extricating himself from too great a proximity to stone walls and trees. And a few years later Lawson Little was to be the cause of the eventual 14-club limit by burdening his caddie with never less than 20 clubs, including a bewildering variety of pitching implements.)

Two more fours followed over that fierce finish and it was left to the rest to try to match Jones's score.

Jones had finished in 75 for a total of 291. Compston, long before, with that 82 in 297. Macdonald Smith came to the last needing a two to tie. Hardly to be expected, and he duly finished in joint second place on 293. So did Leo Diegel, who putted not that well on occasion with both elbows pointing outwards. The 16th finished off his hopes. Where Jones had flipped his ball dead from a bunker for a four, Diegel had a six engraved on his heart. Poor Leo. As he later said: 'They keep on trying to give me the Open Championship but I won't take it.'

Jones, on the other hand, was halfway to the Grand Slam.

But what manner of golfer was he in mid-1930? There is little today of Jones to see on film and few have seen any of it, whereas the swing of a Jacklin, Weiskopf, Miller, Nicklaus or Palmer are still freshly imprinted on the visual memory. To his contemporaries

– and never mind that seven on the 8th at Hoylake – Jones was perfection. Francis Ouimet, the first man to show that US golfers could match others by taking the 1913 US Open in a playoff against Harry Vardon and Ted Ray, thought this of Jones: '. . . he never makes any mistakes. He manages to do everything better than anybody else. He can drive straighter than any man living. He is perfectly machine like in his iron play, and on the greens he is a demon.'

So that's how Jones seemed to Ouimet and most other observers of the day. Yet we have just seen that Jones made mistakes in plenty and was the more fallible the better things were going for him.

In 1977 what follows might be a fair analysis of his abilities as a shotmaker. Let us begin with the fiddly bits. Jones had superb touch and judgement on the long putts. He holed a few but, more important in the long run, he got so many of them to that comfortable distance from the hole at which the golfer feels he has just a formality to complete in knocking it in. For play around the green neither Jones nor anyone else claimed that he was outstanding, yet in his era perhaps no one was. A year or so later Sarazen showed that bunker shots should always be laid somewhere near the hole and today a shot that sets the ball down within a yard is regarded as not exceptional. In Jones's day it was. Certain shots in that category of both Jones and Hagen (a better bunker player anyway) have gone down into the folklore of golf.

The name of Hagen has just been mentioned. He had almost complete mastery of the non-full shots into the green – the short pitch, the little run-up, the chip. Of course, Jones was no slouch in these departments but he was also by no means outstanding. Perhaps he was in the Nicklaus category in these areas. It has been said of Jack that, despite the legends of his power, he is not the best at anything but that when you average it all out he's good at all of it: hits a long ball, is a good iron player, is steady on the shots into the green, and a safe enough putter.

No, the greatness of Jones probably showed in the shots which demand the full golf swing. Probably above all he achieved his reputation for being a 'mechanical golfer' from being both a long and straight driver. Perhaps no one, except Henry Cotton, has found the exact middle of more fairways with less drift from right to left or left to right on his ball. As Cotton has said, when speaking of trick shots, the most difficult trick of them all is to hit a golf ball in a dead straight line. Jones seems to have done this a high proportion of the time, although often with a suggestion of draw on the ball. As regards distance, Jones was longer off the tee than any of his contemporaries – except for the freaks that could lash a ball a long way in no very predictable direction – and was perhaps, on average, the longest hitter of quality using a hickory shaft. Naturally, steel shafts changed all that: many years later Jones himself was to remark of Nicklaus that he played a kind of game with which Bobby was not familiar – such was the difference in length of shot.

Bobby Jones was also in the highest of categories as a long-iron player and with fairway woods. His one weakness on full shots was with what would today be the 'full wedge' and, for Bobby, a full niblick. After he had retired from competitive golf, it was found that his individually-selected clubs formed a perfectly matched set – with the exception of that niblick. It had always given Bobby trouble but in the year of 1930 he found that at last he was hitting that club well too.

And so, a few weeks later to Interlaken for what was really the last great hurdle to the Grand Slam – the United States Open Championship, of which he was already the holder.

After two rounds the leaders formed a kind of roll call of the best American golfers from the mid-20s onwards. Leading was Horton Smith on 142. Closely following, two shots behind, there came the nicely nicknamed Light-Horse Harry Cooper – one of the best golfers never to win an Open – an emigré Englishman Charles Lacey and, of course, Bobby Jones. Within two shots of these were Macdonald Smith, Tommy Armour, Wiffy Cox, Johnny Farrell and Mr Hagen.

Jones had been reserving his best stuff for the third round, though he had already played the most legendary poorish shot he ever hit in the second round. On a par five he was within reach of the green for his second shot. Between him and the green lay a pond and in that pond grew lilies. Jones had selected a spoon for the carry. (Lofts on clubs get progressively more set back. The spoon that Jones used had the loft of a present-day 2 wood (not a 3)). He thinned the shot and the ball flew low towards the water barrier, before skimming across the surface in a series of hops. Lucky? Yes; unusual? Not very. Immediate legend had it that Jones's ball had flipped into a lily pad and bounced from there over the water.

Much relieved, Jones saw his ball come to rest on the bank in front of the green from where he was highly content to flick it to a yard and then sink the putt.

The third round used to be thought the most crucial of a championship though I doubt we think of it in quite these terms today. The idea was that after you had established yourself tidily in the first two you then began to have doubts about the whole enterprise, hence a fading away in round three. But Jones went on to produce his best round of this Championship and one as low as he ever played in an Open.

He went to the turn in 33 and with the 17th and 18th to go had added three more birdies so that there was now a 66 in his sights. But he faltered at the last fences and finished in 68.

This was a performance good enough to jerk him into a five-stroke lead over Light-Horse Harry.

But as I've said earlier, Jones was seldom quite at his best when he had such a lead as this one. He took 75 in the last round but that was amply good enough. Again the par threes had done him little good. He had fives on three of them but there were birdies as well to compensate. Perhaps his last few holes in open championship golf should be recorded: Par 3, 4, 4, 4, 3, 4; Jones 5, 3, 4, 3, 5, 3.

There you have what was unmachinelike about the man: one par, two fives at par threes and three birdies. The last was a fitting way to end a career for a master of the long putt. Jones's second shot came to rest about 15 yards from the hole and then down went the putt.

Of course the Grand Slam was not yet accomplished and neither perhaps was Jones thinking in terms of ending a career. There was the US Amateur Open yet to come and still months away. But this was the one regarded as needing an act of God if Jones was not to win.

In the first round his opponent played as well as any and recorded seven pars and a birdie over the first nine noles. That made him four down and Jones duly ran out the winner. He had gone out in 33. The second time out Jones staggered to the turn in 42 but this time his opponent's play was even less inspired.

When Jones's last championship win came to an end he had never been down to an opponent and the last 36-hole match finished on the 29th green. At the age of 28 Jones then decided to retire. Why he did so is still not entirely clear. In the forefront of his mind was the undoubted fact that there were no more mountains to conquer and his only regret in this respect was that he never dominated an Open from start to finish, remorselessly building a lead of three to five to . . . But then to his contemporaries, win or lose, Jones was always the dominant figure. An offer also came up to make instructional films and, as an amateur, Jones could not do it. There was also the suggestion that he might like to design a set of irons to his own specifications, a very attractive project to him, for this was a man who had built up a set based on his own choice from the best that the forges of Scottish clubmakers could produce. By experience, Jones thought he knew a thing or two about what makes a good golf club. Finally perhaps there was the fact that Jones loved golf as few have done since but he did not love championship golf. He would far sooner play a friendly four-ball with a congenial group than any other form of golf. This love of the game he has in common with Palmer, whereas not a few of today's superstars would be happier at a little hunting or fishing. Nicklaus and Weiskopf, for example.

And so, like the hero of a Western with a job well done, he left the striving for championships and joined Harry Vardon in legend as later have Hogan and Nicklaus.

Face to face

Although matchplay is not dead, in professional golf it is a rare experience for the spectator. Why this should be so, Peter and I discuss in the course of the individual accounts that go to make up this chapter but whatever the reasons may be, just two face-to-face events remain on the professional calendar.

One was the Piccadilly World Matchplay Championship which was immediately popular with the golfing public at its foundation in 1964 and has remained so, indeed increasingly so, ever since. True, towards the end of 1976 the cigarette firm announced that it could no longer afford to sponsor the event but by the autumn of 1977 the name of Colgate was firmly in the gap that Piccadilly's withdrawal left.

The other event's future has been in jeopardy since not long after the Second World War. That one is the Ryder Cup and the problem has been that Great Britain and Ireland has only infrequently seemed credible as opposition to the might of the United States. But perhaps that is not as important as it might seem at first sight. The basic point of the Ryder Cup, especially for the US team, is that it gives golfers an opportunity to represent their country and to be selected is acknowledgement that the particular golfer is amongst the best there is. In this respect, no other of the international events is at all strictly comparable. True there are the arguments that because Britain is no match, at least on average, for the US, there should be a change in the format so that, for example, American golfers would match themselves against the Rest of the World. Yet that would not be a very stirring banner to fight under. OK to play for the World against the Martians but to play for the Rest of anything must always sound a little like the dregs left at the bottom of the coffee cup! Perhaps if there were still a British

Commonwealth that would do well enough as a basis for team selection . . .

So the Ryder Cup will continue, perhaps with minor changes, under the same basic US versus Great Britain system of selection for a good many years yet. Perhaps, in fact, until any one country can claim a consistently better output of golfers than can Britain.

Because of this dearth of matchplay competition it will be no surprise that the World Matchplay and the Ryder Cup are at the centre of this chapter.

Round two

Tony Jacklin played Lee Trevino twice in 1972. Both events would be high up on anybody's list of the great man-to-man encounters of golf history. In July they fought out the Open at Muirfield, watching and matching each other shot for shot as they played round together the final two days. It was perhaps tougher on Jacklin's nerves than Trevino's for this is the Open already a legend for Trevino's holing of everything in sight – particularly if he were off the green, preferably in a bunker.

Jacklin had begun 69, 72 to the American's 71, 70 and had then improved to a 67, during which his fires had been stirred by hitting his second shot at the 558-yard 5th hole to two or three yards and sweeping the putt in. Undeniably that's the ideal way to play a golf hole. Lee Trevino's perfection that day was of a different kind but every bit as effective when it comes to checking what's been written down on the scorecard.

He had gone out in even par – 36 – but it all happened from the 447-yard 14th onwards. On that hole, Trevino hit a 4 iron to within six or seven yards of the flag and sent the putt in. He repeated the performance on the next. Nothing exceptional about that, you may say. They are all supposed to hit a drive down the fairway, send an iron onto the green and hole some of the medium-length putts. True indeed. For the short hole that followed, Trevino decided on a 6 iron, only to find that the leather grip had unwound. Well most American leather grips these days have a gluey backing and all you have to do is grasp the steel shaft firmly and wind it back on. Nevertheless, it's not quite the job one would choose to pass the time when trying to win an open championship. It seems the task did not distract and soothe Trevino. He pushed his tee shot into a bunker to the right of the flag. He was faced with a shot from a downhill lie and with the back lip of the bunker too close to be dismissed from the mind.

'Oh dear,' breathed the gallery. Instead of floating out, Trevino's ball came out low and strong, with enough pace and lack of back-spin to carry on through the green and perhaps leave him with the opportunity of trying to do better next time from a bunker the other side of the green. The ball pitched short of the flagstick, skipped sharply on, hit it in the precise middle and duly collapsed into the hole, all impetus spent. Jacklin's reluctant pencil would have to write down a two, instead of the five he may have begun to have in mind.

Trevino advanced enthusiastically to the next tee, the 542-yard 17th. Afterwards he said, 'I really mellowed the drive. I was swinging at the world. Five iron, two putts, another birdie. On 18 I hit the ball as hard as I could and cut a 5 iron through the green. I chipped 30 feet and when it started rolling I knew it was in. Another birdie. I can't remember ever having five birdies in a row.'

So at the end of that day Trevino was a shot up on Jacklin, four ahead of Doug Sanders, five on Brian Barnes and six on Jack Nicklaus. All the odds were on a gunfight between the two leaders the next day and so it proved. More or less. Nicklaus confused the issue by going out in 32 and then having a couple more birdies. It all meant that he was six under par with four holes to go. But there were no more birdies and he dropped a shot on the 17th to finish with a stirring 66, one of the great rounds of the Open's history and it could have been at least a couple of shots lower.

Trevino and Jacklin, as they played, knew that one of them must win but there was also the thought that Nicklaus was the bear that might hug them both to death. Indeed, after his birdie at the 10th, he did lead the Championship momentarily.

By the time that Jacklin and Trevino stood on the 17th tee, Nicklaus had faltered. Both knew that to beat him they had to finish in level par and gain one shot on each other. Quite a situation.

This time, Trevino did not 'mellow' his drive at all. He pulled his shot into a bunker and had then to watch Jacklin strike long and straight. Jacklin's ball was still ahead of him after the bunker shot and not far behind after Trevino had hit a 3 wood short of the green into long grass. Jacklin failed to reach the green but had only a short pitch left. This pulled up some 15 feet short of the hole but still left him with a fair chance of a birdie. 'Well that's that, I've thrown it away,' Trevino said to his caddie.

Trevino's pitch from the long grass scuttled through the green. He had now to chip and single putt just to get a six. Trevino reached his ball, examined the lie briefly and seemed unconcerned which club he dragged out of his bag. Equally cursorily he glanced towards the hole and then quickly played the shot. For Trevino, the Championship was over. But a horrified Tony Jacklin saw that it was by no means over. Trevino's ball went into the hole. That was a par five, not the certain six and quite possible seven. And Jacklin had now to hole his 15-feet putt in order to draw level with Trevino. 'That,' said Trevino to himself, 'may be the straw that breaks the camel's back.' Perhaps it was. Jacklin's first putt skirted the hole and he had a three-footer return to get in to stay one behind Trevino. By now, the greens were well spiked around the hole for all the final day competitors had passed by. Either a spike mark diverted Tony's short putt or it was never on line for the hole.

Jacklin was a punctured balloon; there was now no hope of winning unless Trevino played the 18th hole more badly than was conceivable. Trevino, full of verve after two gifts from the gods in as many minutes, launched full out into his drive and struck it superbly. Inevitably his following iron shot was to the heart of the green.

Round one to Lee Trevino.

The next round took place on Friday, October 13, some three months later, when the pair met in the semi-finals of the Piccadilly World Matchplay. Both seemed to be at peak form. Trevino, though suffering a virus, had just dealt unkindly with Doug Sanders. In the second round of their 36-hole match he had gone out in 31 and followed that with a two on the 190-yard 10th. Sanders had held on well but in the end lost by two and one. Jacklin had been even more severe. He accounted for Grier Jones by seven and six and must have felt in full command of the

7,000-yard, par 74 Wentworth course – he had won the British PGA there earlier in the season. He had also been thinking, since losing to Trevino at Muirfield. Perhaps the latter's chatter and crowd bantering had disturbed his concentration. He told Trevino that he would rather not talk. Trevino had the appropriate retort: 'I don't care if you don't want to talk. Just listen.' Jacklin's reply, if there was one, has not been recorded.

Both began with a par followed by birdie twos on the 157-yard 2nd hole and Trevino then went one up, only to have his birdie lose the next to Jacklin's eagle. At the turn Trevino was one up having gone out in 32 to Jacklin's 34 but a birdie two from the British player put the match square on the 10th. The cut and thrust continued but after the 14th Trevino held a one-hole lead. The concluding holes of the morning round then just about finished Jacklin off – or so it seemed at the time. He went 5, 4, 6, 5 against Trevino's 4, 4, 5, 4 and that meant three holes lost. And so to lunch, a very indigestible four down.

During the break, Jacklin had another thought. He realized he'd been breaking one of the cardinal laws of the putting stroke. Every putt, however short, must be struck crisply. Tony felt he'd been taking the club back a shade too far and then was slowing up as he came into the stroke. Well all of us are subject to sudden visions of what's wrong with our putting – or indeed just about any other aspect of the game. The crunch comes when you put the new notion into practice. If the first one's good there is more confidence to be poured into the next attempt. If not, it's usually farewell to whatever the new theory was.

Both parred the first three holes and that left Jacklin still four down. Trevino then birdied the 497-yard 4th hole but Jacklin didn't. From about ten yards he sent his putt down for an eagle three. That could have done the theory no harm at all. Jacklin went to the next tee and hit a 5 iron full at the flag. A couple of minutes later down went that putt too and another single putt followed on the next hole. That was as good a spell as you can have without divine intervention in the form of holes in one – four under par for three holes. It also meant that Jacklin was now only one down and the match was wide open once more. At the 8th it was level; again a Jacklin 5 iron flew straight at the flag and finished more or less dead. All square. A hole more, another flawless 5 iron, and Jacklin led for the first time after another birdie.

Trevino had gone out in 35 – one under par – and had lost five of the nine holes played, for Jacklin had needed only 29 shots so far. Trevino then counter attacked over the next three holes with birdie, par, birdie, against Jacklin's par, birdie, par. All square then with six to go. Jacklin's putting continued to serve him well. He missed the 13th green but from off the green putted up stone dead to match Trevino's surer four. On the par-five 15th he followed a weak short pitch by holing from about four yards. Like Jacklin, Trevino had seen his drive finish in the trees but had hit a long fade to the green round them. For a spell, the American had held the edge on the past few holes. Would the 17th again be crucial as at Muirfield? Again there was a par five to be played, measuring 555 yards. Again Jacklin seemed to hold the advantage as he lay far ahead of Trevino after two shots but the American thrust in a low iron shot that came to rest about a yard from the hole. Jacklin's turn now. From about 60 yards his pitch bounced once, hit the flag and stopped a couple of yards away. Halved in birdies and all to play for on the last.

This hole measures about 500 yards and is a dogleg to the right. The tee shot must clear a road and be to the left in order to give an unobstructed shot to the green. Both hit long drives a little too much to the right. They would have to fade into the green. Jacklin hit a straight one and finished about 30 yards left of the flag; Trevino's wood ought by now to be part of golf legend. It slid past the trees, caught the apron of the green and curved towards the hole before finishing about four yards past the hole. Jacklin then chipped well but was Trevino's distance away in one more shot. In the end it was a par five for Jacklin. A four and the match for Trevino.

Wentworth's par of 74 is a little flattering to players: it includes no less than six par fives and of these only the 17th is out of range for most players in two shots. For a long hitter then, the strictest par for the course is 69 but the course is by no means a joy to most of those endowed with the ability to hit a golf ball a long way. The West Course winds among the trees and it is as important to keep the ball out of them as it is to blast it a long way. So if we add a bit on for course difficulty strict par comes out at around 71 or 72. Trevino went round twice in 67 and Jacklin, after opening with 72, followed that with 63 for the afternoon round – and lost. Nevertheless it must rank high among the great rounds of the last decade. Not a bogey on the card, only one five and that glittering first half that included five birdies and an eagle and swept Jacklin from four down to one up.

What Trevino thought about it all when the end had come was not difficult to see. He was able to laugh about it in the Press tent but as he left the last green there was more than a hint of grey in his complexion. Then for him it was bed at nine and the fires burnt out the next day. His calculated fade, in the final against Tom Weiskopf, became as often an uncontrollable slice and Tom took the match by four and three.

The big match

DeWitt Weaver is one of the best of American matchplay golfers. You haven't heard of him? That doesn't surprise me at all, for although Mr Weaver has an enviable record in the miniscule quantity of this kind of golf played in the US he does not otherwise figure in the folklore of golf. For matchplay, if not quite dead, does not kick with a great deal of vigour. There are various reasons for this. For a start, it does not fit in at all well with TV requirements. When the thrusting TV executive is handling sliderule and pencil and involving himself in the complexities of what TV audience is to be expected between three and five on the final afternoon of the US Open or even the Colgate/Benson and Hedges/West of England Open, he has a shrewd idea that there will be a measure of public interest in what is happening : is Nicklaus going to win again? Can Joe Soap maintain his lead? Can Julius Boros/Dai Rees/Dow Finisterwald win at their great ages? And so on.

But in matchplay, all these names may be well on the way back to wherever they came from, ignominiously dismissed by that same Joe Soap in the first round. And whereas it is quite all right to have Joe Soap slugging it out with Jack or Johnny or Gary in the closing moments of a tournament it's really no good at all to have *two* Joe Soaps battling through the final of someone or other's matchplay contest.

Jack, Johnny, Tony, Arnold, Peter – and a host of other first names that you can add the last part to – also do not like matchplay. What *they* do not like about it is being beaten directly and unambiguously by anyone at all. Because anyone can graciously move off from a stroke play tournament making comments about their putting being off and why don't they prepare greens properly in Aberystwyth and anyway the new shaft on my driver did not work out. Somehow any combination or further variety of these remarks sounds more or less entirely reasonable to most of us and no one really feels that X has been defeated by Y but that X just did not happen to be quite on his game that week and, alas, finished 45th.

But matchplay is different. You either beat someone or someone beats you – and never mind your problems with putting and the new driver shaft. Whatever flow of explanation you can summon up, you were *beaten*.

Look at it from another level. One of the stars at my local club is, like the rest of us, invariably 'beaten' in strokeplay competitions. Of course, he does not feel in the least humiliated. He has just not had the best of days and anyway who cares when the winner of the Briggs-Davison trophy was playing off an 18 handicap and managed to scrabble an 84 gross when the course was anyway playing so short? But put that same man onto the arena with that 18 handicapper and let the 18 handicapper win and you then have a different story. There may be clubs flung, uncomplimentary words spoken and a little bit of storming off the course when one has been beaten by six and five.

So one of the few forms of matchplay golf left is the sudden death played out by those tieing for first place in run-of-the-mill strokeplay competitions. Gary Player is very bad at these, on his record a very good bet to lose. Yet, also on his record, the best matchplay golfer of the last decade or so. This, of course, is based on his successes in the Piccadilly World Matchplay, held at Wentworth in Surrey since 1964. But it is what happened in 1965 that is legend and also made Gary Player into a great matchplay golfer, although he does remain one of the worst of playoff protagonists.

It was one of those coppery autumn days when Wentworth looks its best but that 15 October of 1965 Gary Player and his opponent, Tony Lema, had things in mind other than the state of the beech trees. They were concerned with the oft-debated question of the Big Three. Who was in it? Nicklaus definitely and Palmer equally so. The situation was decidedly less clear as regards the Third Man – Player or Lema? And Lema, having won the British Open rather casually in 1964 and nearly having done so the following year was undoubtedly knocking at Player's door. Indeed Player was, that October, feeling a little upset about one commercial judgment that had been made about membership of the Big Three: Slazengers had allowed Gary Player's contract to lapse and had instead signed up Tony Lema worldwide for autographing their clubs and other golf gear.

Their semi-final match began with little hint of the high drama to come. Both parred the first three holes and Player then sent a 4 iron a few yards short of the flag at the 497-yard 4th hole. He got his eagle and that was one up. The position was unchanged at the turn, with Player out in 34 to Lema's 35 against a par of 36. But what you went out in and what you came back in may well not matter in matchplay. A loss is a loss, whether you had a five to your opponent's four or an eight.

The 10th hole was significant in the earlier skirmishing for this 36-hole match. This is a par three of about 190 yards (let us get away from exact measurements of distance which sound scientific but ignore the fact that the length of the hole always depends on where the teeing-off markers are pushed in on a particular day). For a good shot there is no problem on the 10th: your ball is on the green. But if not, there is heather all the way and trees short of it and screening the right-hand half.

Here Player put his 5 iron about three yards away from the flag and it was Lema's turn to see what he could do about that. With the same club, he hit the trees and came down into the uninviting kind of topography that usually tends to be found amongst the roots of trees. Two up to Player? No, Lema got it onto the green and then holed the putt. Player did not get his two but there was a safe three and no great harm done but perhaps a feeling that a very good tee shot had really not been rewarded.

In the immediate future things went like this.

11th   Player in the trees. Had to play out sideways. Lost hole.
12th   Lema on the green of this 480-yard hole with a drive and a 4 wood. Player wasn't.

13th   Player troubled by the rough.
14th   Lema hit a very true 4 iron to two feet.

Without going into too much, for Player, agonizing detail, Tony Lema then birdied the next three holes, while on the 18th, Player holed a putt of about five yards. Well done Gary, that stopped you going in to lunch seven down . . .

Lema had finished his morning's work by recording five birdies in seven holes. Hardly surprising then that he felt no urgent need to visit the practice ground. Player did. He was troubled by a tendency for the ball to draw a little too much towards the end of its flight. The technicalities of weight transfer, getting the hips out of the way early enough, straight through at the target with the hands, and so on, having been satisfactorily adjusted and the appropriate compensations built into the swing, Player was there on the 1st tee as confident as a man may be who stands at six down. He then produced a perfect demonstration snap hook. ('Duck hook' is the usual term but it doesn't approach the impact conveyed by that word 'snap'. Player, or you or I have hit a ball right out of the middle of the club – none of that dragging feeling you get from a slice – and then, as we look up, the thing is curling away low and rapidly, running and running into the middle of all that scenery with which we do not wish to become better acquainted. Better by far the dull pasture before us and the well-mown green in the distance.)

So, seven down with 17 to go. After this nadir of fortune, a ray of light promising a distant glimpse of self respect followed. Player got a two on the 155-yard 2nd and then birdied the next. Five down. The 4th was halved and Player then grabbed yet another hole back with a birdie two on the 190-yard 5th. That one was rather too close, however. Lema had been about ten yards away with his tee shot, but his putt had hit the hole and then spun away.

So for Player the skies were, in such a short space of time, detectably bluer – three down and far from home is by no means an insurmountable hill to climb.

The 6th at Wentworth is very much the shortest par four on the course at around 340 yards but you must keep your tee shot to the left as the fairway doglegs gently right. If you have done that part of it adequately, you have then only to pitch your ball on with whatever you fancy. Both did so and Lema secured his four without difficulty. Would Player get his putt down for a three? He went at it with confidence and the intent not to be short. It did not go in but stopped only two feet past. Gary missed the return. At that point the match ought to have been over for in any matchplay confrontation confidence soars as the holes start to come back. But once let this exciting flow be impeded and total despair is likely to be immediate and final. So there was Gary suddenly not with a birdie putt in the hole and a mere two down but a missed par and four down, which was, in terms of the number of holes left to play, worse than his position on the 1st tee after lunch.

Gary Player has said that this Lema match 'contains my whole life story', by which he means fighting against adversity of various kinds and he further claims that at this point he became not so much downcast as 'supercharged'. But the results did not show at all immediately. Three halved holes followed and the last of these required Player to get the ball into the hole from about five yards to avoid a loss.

At the par-three 10th, Player was happy enough to see Tony Lema miss the green and that was a hole back. At the 11th, Player sent his ball nicely down the middle, pitched to a yard or so and then holed the putt. Perhaps now there were a few doubts in Tony Lema's mind, but three up with seven to go is a position that any world-class golfer thinks he is unlikely to relinquish. The 12th was halved and then Player, with the honour on the next drove straight. Lema did not; he hooked into the bushes, was duly thankful to find his ball, but could do no more than knock it out. Player hit a mid-iron to the green and his ball came to rest about three yards from the hole. Lema, in three, was on the front edge and it was therefore his putt. He holed it and Player now, on the instant, had to get down in one, not two, for a win. But he did it.

There is a saying in golf's vocabulary, that two up with five to go never wins. Certainly poor Hale Irwin, playing almost faultless golf, lost against David Graham in the 1976 Piccadilly. This was Lema's status and I doubt that he would have wished the mathematics to be reversed. Better still for Tony when the 14th and 15th were halved and there's certainly no saying that two up with three to go does not win.

At the 16th it matters very little who hits the longest drive. The aim is to keep out of trouble. But Player, instead of using a 1 or 2 iron from the tee, decided to see if there was anything in the psychology of getting a long one straight down the fairway. He managed that and then stood aside for Lema to follow it.

Lema had been driving with a 3 wood in order to keep out of the trees that flank nearly every fairway at Wentworth. Perhaps, as Player thinks, as a result of going for length, he hooked it. He had to hit another one from that tee and Player was now in the position of being one down with two to go.

The 17th at Wentworth is one of the great par fives of golf. For the solid hitter it is entirely possible to get home in two shots but both of them must be bold and challenge disaster. The drive must be held to the left and that is where the out-of-bounds fence is. That out-of-bounds has cost many a two-stroke penalty over the years. If a good drive has been hit, a second driver shot may still be needed to reach the green. It must be accurate as well as powerful to avoid the trees, and ground to the right of the green falls away dangerously to the woods.

Neither Lema nor Player did reach in two. Player, however, was just a handful of yards short whereas Lema had a full pitch to play. He sent it to about four yards and Player chipped inside him to a yard or so nearer. The American's nerve held and he got the putt in; Player had his three yarder not to lose the match. He got it and stood one down with the 500-yard 18th remaining.

Both drove securely down the middle but Lema then hit a near hook which came to rest about 50 yards short. Player took a 4 wood and just skirted the trees. His ball stopped some four yards from the pin. Lema had to get his little pitch close but his ball stopped well short of the hole: he had forgotten that there was now the dampness of evening in the air and on the green. The match was level. They made their way to the 1st tee once again.

The players drive over the approach road to the clubhouse and try to keep left as this position opens up the shot to the green. The second has to carry a deep dip and a steep slope up to the green, which is crowned and well protected by bunkers, trees and bushes. Again Lema's tendency to hook found him out and he was bunkered to the left of the green. Player made no mistake. The match was over.

Player found the fact that he could now relax was too much for him and he passed out. When he shortly came to, he found himself crying and trembling. Lema's feelings are not recorded.

The standard of golf was not by any means at the superb level of the Jacklin v Trevino encounter described elsewhere. There holes changed hands as a result mostly of birdies and eagles. What really happened was that Lema went round the first 18 in 67 and secured his landslide lead at lunchtime as a result of coming back in 32 against par of 38. In terms of sheer scoring, Player then dominated by covering the 19 holes after lunch in 70.

Player had already won each of the major championships (including the US Open earlier in 1965) and he went on to defeat Peter Thomson, holder of the British Open, in the matchplay final the next day. This was his first of five victories in this Championship. Such has his dominance been in this event that, however much he may happen to be complaining of duck hooking, poor putting and other such dire ailments, he is always the favourite. When indeed Hale Irwin had a narrow lead in the 1974 final, everyone *knew* Gary was going to come storming back. Of course he would – hadn't he come back from seven down in 1965? Did not he again and again manage to get down in two from bunkers against Graham Marsh of Australia before winning on the 40th hole? But history does not always repeat itself. Against Irwin, Player suddenly missed a short return putt and that was virtually the end of the match.

The man who lost the Ryder Cup

There are more ways than one to join the immortals. No one, for instance, can compare with Sam Snead for the sheer length of time the man has played golf of unsurpassed quality. Forty glorious years at the top when putting stroke, precision and power have for most major golfers long departed before they even reach that age. Yet Snead is remembered particularly for two things: an unmatched swing, and failure in the US Open Championship. Never mind that he won the British once, and the US PGA and the Masters three times each. What matters more to the Press and, as a result, the Public, is that his achievements in the US Open were very clearly a good deal less glorious than his swing. Many times, it seems, Sam has hurled his ball away into convenient undergrowth or water hazard after one three putt too many for his composure. More remembered by far, however, are the two occasions when he threw not his ball but an Open away at the last gasp. The first of these was in 1939 when Sam amassed an eight on the last hole. It was quite a good eight really, as eights go. He compiled it thinking he needed a birdie to tie for first place, whereas just a par would have made him the outright winner. Those playing with him knew this but were concerned to observe the rule that you don't tell a player he has 'only' anything at all to get. So Sam went full out at a succession of shots that went nowhere very encouraging – including one that ended in a crack in a bunker face. Never mind, Sam was young. Doubtless he'd win it in a year or two.

The second legendary failure came in 1947. Lew Worsham and Snead had each to hole putts of some two and a half feet to win. Snead saw clearly that his was a touch longer than Worsham's. He began to line himself up and Worsham then demanded that the putts be measured. They were, and Snead then duly missed. Worsham pushed his in and that was the end of poor Sam for ever, as far as the US Open is concerned.

Sam does not much care to be reminded of either of these events, which he thinks of as isolated incidents in a career that has included seven major championships and more than a hundred tournament wins. Peter Alliss has been reminded more times than he cares to remember, and far more than mortal man can count, of how he lost the 1953 Ryder Cup. Several millions, it must be, were there and every one of them is willing to give Peter a vivid description of what he saw that day.

In the singles on the last day at Wentworth the 22-year-old Alliss was drawn against one of the multitude of Turnesa brothers. Jim it was this time and by far the weakest member of the US Ryder Cup team – so everyone said. Alliss was bound to win against such a non-superman. Alliss went round in 70, four shots below par and that left him one down at lunch. The ageing Turnesa was having a good day.

Little chance anyway was being given to the British team. They had lost the previous day's foursomes by three matches to one and this was the form of contest in which they were thought to have the best chance because British players are supposed to have more experience of alternate-shots golf. Surely they would be destroyed in the singles? Alliss had already had a foretaste in those foursomes of how imminent success in golf can recede very sharply indeed.

On the 35th hole, the only strict par five on the West Course, the US pairing of Johnny Douglas and Ed 'Porky' Oliver had put their tee shot encouragingly out of bounds. Their one-up position ought to deteriorate rapidly to all square with one to play. The British pairing of Peter Alliss and Harry Weetman, barring one – or perhaps two – miracles, had now 'only' to get down in five to win the hole. Weetman was perhaps the mightiest smiter of a golf ball in the history of British golf. Having been no doubt much comforted by the American tee shot, he set himself to deliver a fearsome blow. His shot was straight, but straight up rather than straight along. It carried about 150 yards, about the distance Harry would reckon normally to achieve with a gentled sand wedge. Alliss had no chance at all, of course, to reach the green and decided, after consultation with Harry, that the sensible thing to do was push a 5 iron towards the green across the out-of-bounds fence and leave Harry to play a medium-length iron to the green. Peter did his part safely and Harry then thinned the approach shot across the green and beyond. Meanwhile the Americans had been improving. They lay eight feet from the hole after five shots. Alliss pitched to four feet, the Americans holed out, Weetman missed.

Weetman's play the next day also did the illustrious name of Alliss no good at all. He became one of the homeland heroes without any conspicuous achievements on his part becoming necessary. Snead was there and at this time most people thought that a match against Snead was a match lost. With five holes left to play the Weetman v Snead match was clearly over. Snead was four up, in that reassuring position where you know that all you have to do is hit one, or at the most two, shots at the flag to win. Weetman played no more than steadily thereafter; Snead, perhaps too much relaxed by thoughts of inevitable victory, used the lazy elegance of his swing to hit most of his final shots deep into the woods. Well done Harry, and suddenly the burden of victory or defeat was squarely on the shoulders of British youth in the persons of Peter Alliss and Bernard Hunt.

We left Peter departing for lunch one down. After the 15th of
the afternoon round he was one up. Alliss, in his own opinion, then
proceeded to lose the match on the next hole though legend has
concentrated far more on the cockpit of the 18th green. Turnesa
sliced wildly to, rather than into, the woods on the 16th. However
much a gentleman he may have been, it could not have been dis-
couraging to have hit a woman and stayed out of the spruce birch.
He followed by hitting into a bunker short of the green. After a
good enough drive Alliss hit his pitch at this 380-yard hole dead
on the flag but it bit rather too sharply and pulled up about 15
yards short of the flag. Turnesa played a competent bunker shot to
ten feet and holed his putt. Alliss had putted up to two and a half
feet. After Turnesa was safely in the hole, Alliss missed. All square
with two to play.

The 17th at Wentworth has that out of bounds on the left that
causes players to be a little cautious with their tee shots. Ideally,
the drive should soar down the lefthand side and it will then kick
with the slope towards centre fairway. From there the green is
open to the second shot. Too far right and there is little chance of
reaching it.

Alliss decided boldly to try to skirt the out of bounds and rely
on his fade to bring the ball back to the fairway. The shot looked
good but it did not drift back enough and finished two feet out of
bounds. Turnesa played cautiously for his par five; Allis contrived a rousing four with his second ball but that meant a six and
Great Britain one down with one to go.

The 18th is a par-five dogleg to the right of about 500 yards. The
drive should be kept to the left, for this line allows both a sight of
the green and a long iron to be played. If you go right, a long faded
wooden-club shot becomes necessary. Turnesa did not manage
anything at all in the way of placement. His slice curved some 50
yards into the woods. Much encouraged, Alliss placed his drive
perfectly. A little later, Turnesa emerged from the trees and
followed up with a third shot to a short-pitch length of the green.
Meanwhile Alliss hit a 2 iron nearly pin high and about 25 yards
left of the flag and some ten yards off the green. A five ought to be
good enough to win the hole and halve the match. No doubt that a
four would do it. Turnesa pitched up to holeable distance. Alliss
had then to go for a four. The safe shot was to take something like a

5 iron – or even a putter – and shove the thing out of the hollow and towards the flag. But from that position a little too much depends on the luck or ill-luck of the bounce. Peter felt he might finish dead or ten feet away. He selected a pitching wedge, to play from the soggy ground with the aim of floating it out of the hollow to bite and stop near the flag.

Behind him was a stand and a lot of shoes. No, there was no chance that he would catch anything on the backswing but . . . With that sort of thought on their minds, golfers both great and small tend to tap a golf ball with less than the ultimate in precision. Peter's shot finished still a yard or so short of the putting surface. Away with the wedge, and he ran it up to about a yard. Turnesa then missed his putt for a five and Peter, in effect, had 'this one for the Ryder Cup'. It didn't go in.

Minutes later Bernard Hunt arrived on the same green and had two putts to win his match. He took three. British youth had failed. We had crowned a queen, climbed Mount Everest and won the Ashes that year but the Ryder Cup, as usual, went back to the US.

Curiously, Hunt's failure to get down in a couple of putts did not go down in golfing legend. Allis was the man blamed; Weetman, the man who had certainly not snatched a victory but had been presented with it, was the hero of the hour.

Yet over the passage of time Peter Alliss built a record in Ryder Cup matches that has not been bettered – though the legend of how he lost it with that fluffed chip and missed putt at Wentworth in 1953 dominates the public memory more than the later victories and hard-fought halves.

In the immediate future Alliss's game went into a decline. Although it's no hanging offence to hit one poor chip and one putt that fails to dive into the hole, memory and frequent reminders from those who claimed they had been there on the day made it seem so. Nineteen fifty-five was another Ryder Cup year. The first seven in the team were automatic selections on a points system based on tournament performance. For the three remaining places two distinctly middle-aged players – Johnny Fallon and Arthur Lees – were selected, together with the highly-combative Eric Brown. Alliss was not; in the tears of the moment he vowed never to play in the damned thing again.

However, when the event returned to Britain in 1957 at Lindrick he was selected and by then was thought of as the best we had to offer. Paired with Bernard Hunt, he lost to Doug Ford and Dow Finsterwald, who returned the useful score of seven under level fours. At the end of the first day Great Britain had lost three four-somes and won one.

I remember that I had bought a ticket for the second and final day and thought I might as well go along and watch the inevitable happen. After all, I might see something that would rub off on a handicap golfer. But there was not the promise of glory to rouse one early from bed and I arrived late in the morning. What had been happening? The scoreboard showed that just about every British player was in the lead! Well, let's go and see how Dai is getting along now against Ed Furgol of the shrunken left arm but a recent holder of the US Open nevertheless. Dai Rees was in fact doing so well that the match was hardly worth more than a few minutes. Furgol had all the air of a man wholly demoralized and eager to be on a different edge of the Atlantic. On then to Peter Mills v the US captain, Jackie Burke. Well that one was not long in the balance either. Thoughts of connoisseurship could now be allowed to intrude. Which players would be presenting the most delectable swings for the education of a club golfer? We were deprived of the awesome slashing of Harry Weetman. He was smouldering in his tents away from the field of battle. Captain Dai Rees had dropped him for the singles the night before and Harry had declared he would never play under Rees again. Neither Hogan nor Snead had been picked and it could indeed be argued that this was the weakest US team that had competed, whereas the British was arguably the best we've put out.

Well, Alliss of course must be watched, though it was a pity he'd been drawn against Fred Hawkins who, the Press said, was the weakest in the US team. Peter had been told much the same thing in both his Ryder Cup matches to date: Cotton had thought little of Jim Turnesa and this time Rees was as slighting of Hawkins.

In the morning Alliss had gone round Lindrick in 70 to stand one up only. As the afternoon wore on and the US team as a whole began to find pars increasingly difficult to get and eventually collapsed almost to a man, Hawkins played just about the best golf of the lot. As the two stood on the 13th tee, Peter still held a one-hole lead and moved along the fairway with head held arrogantly high to a cast-iron four.

(Some golfers love an audience, others do not. Palmer, for instance, seems almost to look intently into the eyes of every member of his gallery within range and had the apocryphal reputation of getting more birdies when the TV cameras were looking at him than when they were switched off. Others snap at caddies, swear none too quietly to themselves, speak brusquely to spectators and slam clubs on ground and into bag until the TV towers come in sight. On the instant, they are all manly determination with a dash of boyish charm, while a rueful shake of the head is the most extreme gesture they will allow themselves. Alliss, he says, had that arrogant-seeming posture because he was shy: with nose tilted an inch or so skywards his gaze would travel over everybody's head and without eye contact unwelcome conversation does not flow, particularly important that day perhaps, when there would have been a few thousand present quite willing to express the friendly hope that he wasn't about to lose the Ryder Cup *again*.)

Hawkins played the hole less surely but, alas for Alliss, steered a long putt home to halve it. He then put the match all square by birdie-ing the par-five 14th. On the long 16th Hawkins got on in two and Peter did not. One down with two to go. Never mind, on the 17th Hawkins had the shot to the green first and finished short. Alliss set himself for the counter blow.

All day Max Faulkner, who had said he ought to be dropped for the singles matches, had swept energetically about the course spreading news, joy, comfort and exhortation alike around the British players. As his match finished, captain Rees had joined in with equal verve. So also Eric Brown who, having won the honour on the 1st tee for his match against short-fused Tommy Bolt had been greeted with the remark 'You're beat sucker'. This did nothing at all to dampen Brown's aggressive instincts and he had won his match comfortably far from home.

Even before this contest began there had been ill feeling between the two. When both were a little late on the tee it was said they were still on the practice ground 'throwing golf clubs at each other from 50 paces'.

Bolt's best days were mainly before the arrival of TV, when spirited club-throwing and breaking was more regarded as evidence of a finely-tuned temperament and the will to win than would be the case today. There is an often-told story about Tommy that will perhaps stretch to one more telling. One day he found himself deliberating choice of club for a shot of some 120 yards. He asked his caddy for an opinion, expecting to be advised to 'hit a full wedge at the flag', 'spare a 9 iron', or 'why not give it just the gentlest little push with a 6, Mr Bolt?'. In the event, he was handed a 2 iron. Tommy protested that in the first flush of youthful strength he certainly agreed he no longer was but his 2 irons were likely to fly a hundred yards, give or take a few, past the flag on a shot like that for a few more years yet. The caddie pointed out that in view of the sheer persistence of destruction Tommy had wrought on his golf armoury there remained little scope for choice . . . but there was still a driver in sound condition . . . ?

Alliss's preparations for a shot that ought to have him all square with one to play were interrupted. 'Never mind, Peter,' it was said, 'it's all over. We've won.' Dai Rees's words were highly welcome to Peter – after all he couldn't now lose the Ryder Cup – but they did nothing at all for his concentration on the immediate task of getting the ball onto the green and going on to beat or halve with Fred Hawkins. Alliss hit it partway under a hedge and duly became the only British player that day to lose. And as for Peter's Ryder Cup record, it now stood: played four, lost four. Things at least had little scope for becoming worse.

Peter considers that the current crop of British golfers are a fairly lowly bunch. True there is Jacklin, one of the best strikers of a golf ball of this or any other era, but . . . And at the opposite pole, Peter Oosterhuis, who surely can't continue indefinitely to get those par-saving putts into the hole. Now if you could get Jacklin to do the long shots, and leave Oosterhuis with the task of scraping it out of unfriendly places onto the green and then to knock the ball into the hole, you might have the best golfer ever. For the rest, it is difficult to say an enthusiastic word for many, once you've considered the virtues of Coles, Gallacher and Barnes.

But in the 1959 Ryder Cup Alliss was paired for the foursomes with a golfer for whom he had, and has, admiration – Irishman Christy O'Connor. Christy, Peter thinks, was (and almost still is) a world beater with, alas, lack of flow on the putting stroke but the ability to play every other shot in golf.

Together they went out against Doug Ford and Art Wall and cruised home quite comfortably, after a few early alarms, by three and two. Who would Alliss get in the singles? Well once again someone they all said was 'not very good really. You oughtn't to have much trouble beating him'. Jay Hebert, it was, though he was not that bad, winning as he did the US PGA the following year. Of course Hebert proved to be quite good, no one who gets into the US Ryder Cup team is less than that. When they came to the last hole Alliss stood one down. This was a par five with water hazards to both left and right. Hebert disappeared from public view and Alliss could now halve his match if he could get the ball onto the green. He hit a 3 iron that was very straight indeed and ended in mid green. A win for the hole, and a halved match. The record now looked considerably better for at the Eldorado Country Club in California Alliss had, with O'Connor in the foursomes, contrived one and a half points. So what, you may say. So Peter had one and a half points against his name and that compared well with the British team's total of three and a half.

It was indeed a turning point. However you explain the thing, Peter *ought* to have got down in three at Wentworth in 1953 on the last and it couldn't have been encouraging to him or anyone else that he had been the sole loser in the singles at Lindrick. But suddenly Alliss was a winner and from this point on he became a man to count on in the British Ryder Cup team. Suddenly also he was no longer to be faced in the singles by players that everyone felt he 'ought to beat'.

In 1961 Arnold Palmer was the opponent. But first, under the changed format, with Christy O'Connor he beat Doug Ford and Gene Littler. Jay Hebert then appeared once again and O'Connor and Alliss found themselves all square with only the last to play. Hebert had a putt of around eight yards to at least halve the match, after which Peter would have to see what he could do from a couple of feet or so nearer the whole. Hebert in unlikely style got his in; Peter did not.

Now, for the first time, Peter had a confrontation to stir the emotions: it was with Arnold Palmer. At the time, Palmer held the British Open, had recently relinquished the US Open and had twice taken the Masters. Nicklaus had not yet fully arrived on the stage and no one therefore had any doubt at all that Palmer was the greatest around. Peter says that he was nervous at the prospect but 'in a definite and positive way'. The match that ensued has since become recognized, like a Cole Porter tune and lyric or a Sinatra interpretation, as a classic of the art of golf matchplay.

The 1st at Royal Lytham and St Anne's measures out at a touch over 200 yards. Both Palmer and Alliss hit good 4 irons onto the green and two-putted. First blood to Palmer followed quickly. After both were short at the 2nd Palmer got a putt in and Alliss did not. The 3rd at Lytham is about 450 yards and that day was playing into a stiff breeze. Alliss had to use a wood for his second shot and did not quite reach the green. Palmer, a savage man with a long iron, hit one with great verve but a lot further away from the green. This time it was Peter who got it into the hole in two more while Palmer did not. Cut and thrust and much the same at the next, where both played wedge seconds and Alliss's came down and stopped a lot nearer the hole. One up to Alliss. Halves at the next two holes and so to the 550-yard 7th, into that day's breeze a par five for everyone. Both struck two good shots and had crisp pitches left to play. Alliss tried to swing his ball in towards the hole from a bank, without success. He chipped up close. Palmer went through the green but held the apron, from where he proceeded to put into the hole. At the 10th, a short par four, Palmer chipped in for a birdie, having again been too strong with his approach. Alliss was already almost dead after his approach shot but certainty tends to feel less sure when suddenly you have to dot the 'i'. However, Peter placed the dot correctly and so retained his one-up position. The next four holes were halved, with Alliss producing one particular shot of great quality. Bunkered from the tee at the par-four 13th, Peter hit an 8 iron from the hard sand full to the green and that was a half when the odds were against.

At the 15th, a long par four, Palmer bunkered his second shot, while Alliss was nearly dead in three. He was still nearly dead after Palmer had sent his sand wedge into the hole at some speed on the second bounce. All square and Palmer had now been down in one three times from off the green. If that particular brand of magic were to rub off on Peter – just the once would probably do it – that would be a first and famous victory in the Ryder Cup singles.

On the next two holes both had equal chances for birdies and all four putts missed. They came to the last all square. Both had 9 irons into the green: Palmer from the fairway after a long drive, Peter from the semi-rough after allowing for his usual fade that this time did not come off. After the two approaches Palmer was about five yards from the hole, Alliss, alas, about the same distance short of the green with the hole looking rather a long way away, set as it was at the back. There were perhaps 40 yards to go and Alliss now felt determined not to lose to a par four on the last. Disgrace was more to be avoided than anything else in Ryder Cup singles. 'I must make him have to get a birdie to win,' Alliss told himself. The resolution held up very well indeed. Peter's pitch and run looked as if it might rabbit into the hole all the way, but in the end it hit the edge and spun a foot or two away. Palmer conceded the putt and went boldly for victory with his. Joy for Peter. It stopped two and a half feet past, the sort of putt that Peter was reputed to miss all too frequently himself and which had cost him his 1953 Wentworth Ryder Cup match. Palmer, looking baleful, crouched over it and locked into his knees-together putting stance. Peter felt perhaps a little too pleased that he hadn't lost and suddenly had the impulse to tell Arnold Palmer to pick it up. The words came out and Palmer obeyed very quickly indeed.

Michael Hobbs was watching and breathed a lengthy sequence of rude words to himself that were less than complimentary about Peter's magnanimity, but the gallery around were breathing differently. 'Jolly sporting,' and the like was the sort of thing they were saying. Probably Peter was right. If Palmer had missed the putt, the result of the match would not have been greatly affected – say Great Britain ten, USA 14, instead of the nine and a half, $14\frac{1}{2}$ eventual result. And then a few years later Jacklin and Nicklaus arrived on the last green to a similar situation and this time it was Nicklaus who told Tony to pick it up. The occasion was far more stressful. Jacklin had to hole his short one not to lose the Ryder Cup. Perhaps Peter's generosity had rubbed off.

Eventide and the grace of Tony Lema

Peter Oosterhuis in the wind

Bob Goalby and Roberto de Vicenzo at Augusta

In sand: Severiano Ballesteros, Tony Jacklin,
Tom Weiskopf and Neil Coles

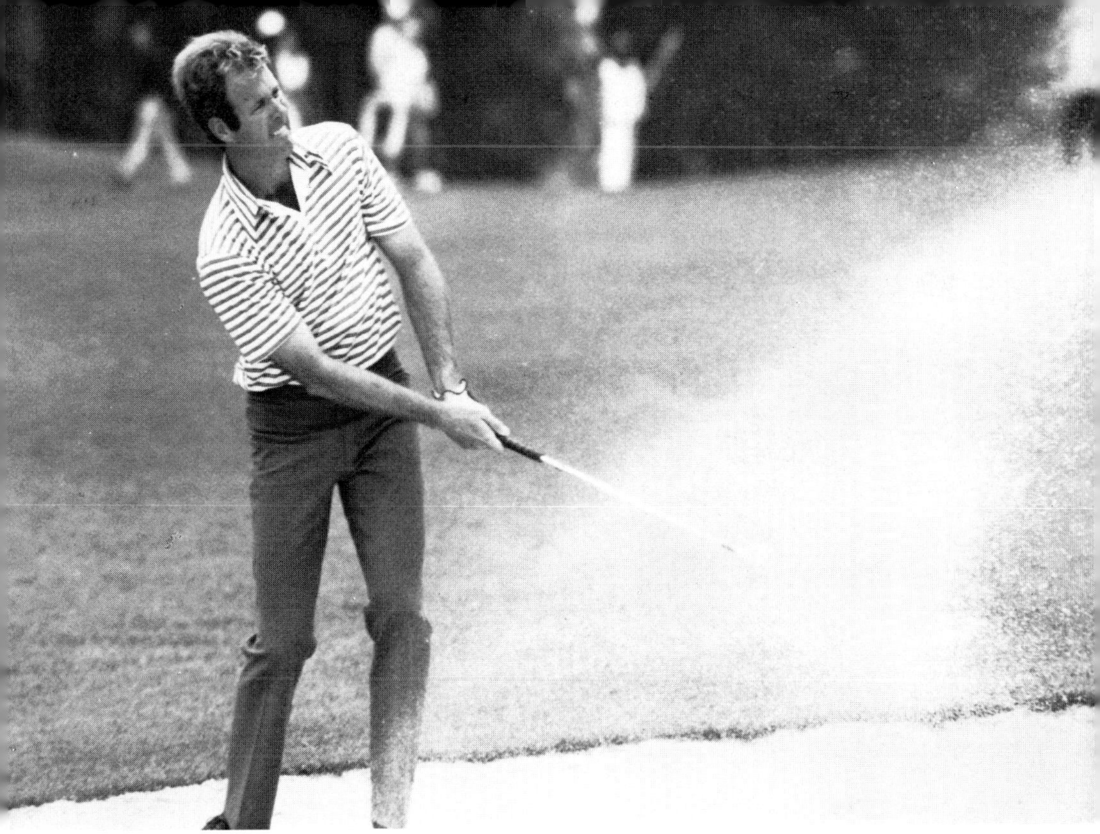

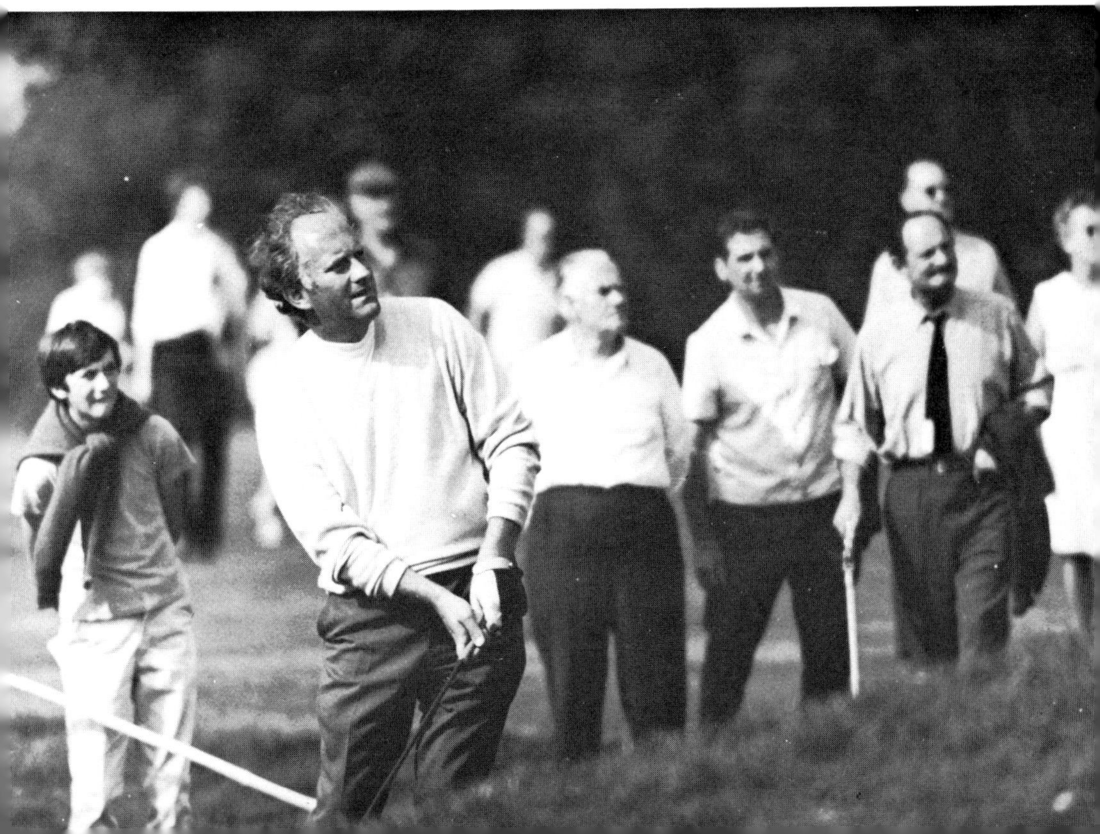

Future superstars? Jerry Pate, 1976 US Open Champion,
and Mark James, British Open Champion 19 . . .?

Wentworth: Graham Marsh in play, Weiskopf watches

The 16th green at Augusta during the Masters

Nineteen sixty-one was, for the Ryder Cup, a point of departure: the format had been changed and was to be changed again, the second time even more in favour of the Americans. Britain, from year to year, can never hope to put forward more than say four players with a real hope, whatever the form of golf, of beating the best four that the US can choose. An in-form Brian Barnes, for instance, may do the unimaginable and beat Nicklaus twice in a day as he did in 1975; but the lightning is highly unlikely to strike the whole team, especially when there are two or three in it who must know that they are not as good as anyone in the top 60 on the US tour. The more the number of matches is increased, the less likely a British victory becomes and the less remembered are outstanding individual matches.

In the foursomes on the first day the British pair of O'Connor and Alliss played poorly enough to go out in 42. In the four-ball series, this time with Hunt, Alliss lost to Tony Lema and Johnny Pott on the last green and they later halved with Julius Boros and Gene Littler.

Then it was Palmer again. The venue was again a historic one: the East Lake course at Atlanta, Georgia, where Bobby Jones learned to play golf. Peter was far from his best and remembers that he was hitting short, cutty little drives that took him not more than a couple of hundred yards up the fairways. The iron shots that followed, however, were of finer stuff. After seven holes Peter would have been three up but for missing putts of five, four and two feet yet remembers that he putted steadily that day. But not all his drives were as short as 200 yards. At the 515-yard 9th he got a good one away and won the hole with a four. At the 12th, the putter worked well and a ten-feet putt fell for a win but a far shorter one missed the hole a little later. On the 483-yard 15th Palmer was in trouble. He hooked from the tee and then bunkered his second shot. Alliss was able to take the hole with a par. At the 16th Alliss missed the green with his long second but Palmer was safely on, only to send his first putt a couple of yards past the hole. But he holed the next for a win and Peter had to halve the last two holes to remain one up. The 17th at East Lake is 410 yards. Alliss sent a 6 iron to the green, about five yards from the hole. Palmer followed him in with a match-winning iron to a yard and suddenly the crowd were yelling. All square coming to the last? No. Alliss got his long putt down and Palmer had now to hole his to stay in the match. He did so.

The last hole at East Lake is a long par three – 230 yards. Palmer still had the honour and hit one straight at the flag but his ball ran about eight yards past. Peter at least had to get his onto the green. He did so, but his ball was a very long way off indeed. He was faced with a curling 20-yard putt. Many golfers are more frightened at the thought of missing a short one than at the prospect of laying a long one comfortably close to the hole but at least you can lock yourself rigid for a short putt and give the thing a stiff prod towards the hole. That sort of stroke never does for a long curler. Delicacy and sureness of touch are what is needed. A much-relieved Alliss saw his ball travelling at about the right pace and a likely-looking line. It stopped a couple of inches from the hole and Palmer knocked it away.

Alliss could not now lose but if Palmer could get his birdie putt in that would be a half. The boldest putter of his generation, Palmer left it a good four feet short.

What was by now the old firm of Alliss and O'Connor turned up again for the 1965 Ryder Cup at Royal Birkdale. In the first four-somes they played steadily and when the match ended they were one under par while Don January and Ken Venturi had lost by five and four. In the afternoon the pace hotted up. O'Connor and Alliss got to the turn in only 31 shots against a par of 35 but Billy Casper and Gene Littler were putting up a far sterner fight than had the first pair of Americans. They took only 32. When the match ended, Peter and Christy were six under par and had won by two and one.

And so to the four-balls the next morning, and the familiar face of Arnold Palmer, who was paired with Dave Marr. The British pairing played steadily but it was not good enough by far. Palmer and Marr won by five and four and the match was repeated after lunch. This time it was far more of a contest. The British got to the turn in 34 and came back in the same number, four under par for the nine holes. Playing the 513-yard last hole the match stood all square. Alliss then played a great 4 wood second to 12 feet. Victory by one hole.

In the singles, Peter's opponents did not include Palmer but

Casper and Venturi were golfers who would be expected to test him. Billy Casper was the morning opponent. Alliss was out in 32 to the American's 33 and came back in 36, again one fewer than Casper managed. The match ended on the last green, with Alliss having to hole from five feet to win and doing so. In the afternoon, Alliss and Ken Venturi matched each other stroke for stroke and both turned in 34. Thereafter Alliss pulled away from the 1964 US Open Champion and took the match three and one.

Great Britain lost the match as a whole quite comfortably by $12\frac{1}{2}$ to $19\frac{1}{2}$. But for Alliss the occasion was a personal triumph. He had got five of those points and his performance was very much better than that of any other British player. At the end of it all his Ryder Cup record as a whole was the best that a British player had achieved, if we exclude the golfer or two who has competed just once or twice and won. Alliss had taken part in six Ryder Cup series, had played 13 singles and won seven of them.

This year was certainly the high-water mark of Peter's Ryder Cup career, which was ultimately to stretch from 1953 to 1969. Could Wentworth now be forgotten? For Peter that particular cross to bear was no more but there was no perceptible slackening in the numbers of those who would edge up to him in golf club-houses throughout the land and remark that they had been at Wentworth that day in 1953.

Alliss played in two more Ryder Cups. The 1967 series was held at the Champions Club at Cypress Creek, about 30 miles out of Houston in Texas. In practice Alliss was the most impressive of the British team – but then he always was . . . In the foursomes, O'Connor again partnered him and they had a solid record behind them of five victories. This time they faced Arnold Palmer and the man who always modelled both his swing and personal appearance on Ben Hogan – Gardner Dickinson. At the turn it was level, then the US took the 10th and 11th before O'Connor put a telling pitch to within a yard at the 14th, thus getting the British pair back into the match. But there came a master stroke at the next and it was not played by either of the British pair. Dickinson had strayed with his tee shot and it looked as if Alliss and O'Connor were about to get the match square again. Palmer was behind a tree. He might play out to the fairway or attempt to play a hook round the tree.

Now there are usually gasps and ecstatic applause when any maestro takes wood in hand and hits either long fading or drawn shot to a far-distant green. But in fact any low-handicap golfer should fancy his chances of bringing off such a coup. As Henry Cotton has said, the most difficult long shot to hit is a dead straight one. But the more loft there is on the club, the more difficult it becomes to fade or hook at will with the ball beginning to curve at just the right moment, particularly when there is something at stake. Palmer selected a 6 iron and brought it off to perfection; Gardner Dickinson followed by sinking the putt. It meant a swing of two holes. Alliss and O'Connor became two down instead of all square. Palmer's shot had given his pairing the match. There was no further exchange of holes and the US ran out the winners by two and one.

And so to the four-balls, Alliss once more playing with Christy O'Connor. But first there was a minor distraction. Alliss's caddie turned up drunk in the morning and, though by no means puritanical in these matters, Peter felt he had to sack him. After all, it was a moot point whether the man was capable of moving himself around the course, let alone carry a standard vast golf bag as well. The British pair then lost by three and two to Casper and Gay Brewer.

By now, barring miracles – and Lindrick is likely to happen but once in a lifetime – the match was lost. There remained only the singles and the British team were already dispirited. However, Peter did not have to concern himself with whether or not he would be playing someone that he would be told was 'no good. You're sure to beat him.' No American is to be despised on home soil. Casper it was. After a close match Peter lost by two and one.

His final opponent was Gay Brewer, perhaps a faded figure today but in 1967 the current Masters champion. Although the match was by now over, there was still the matter of self respect and making the British score look less puny. Alliss won by two and one but Great Britain and Ireland still lost the Ryder Cup once more, this time by a humiliating margin: US 21, GB six. The only hero was David Thomas, while Tony Jacklin had done well enough in his first Ryder Cup.

Peter had now experienced a very full range indeed of Ryder

Cup encounters, from the personal humiliation of Wentworth, to being dropped the next time around and then the high drama of the sudden British ascendency at Lindrick. But the 1969 match was in many ways the most dramatic of all.

By this time Peter was amongst the elder statesmen of British golf and had been overtaken as the leading British player by Tony Jacklin, who came to the next venue, Royal Birkdale, as the first home-grown open champion since Max Faulkner.

Once more it was Alliss and O'Connor in the foursomes and again they gave good account of themselves, halving with Billy Casper and Frank Beard. The next day, Alliss partnered Brian Barnes in the four-balls and faced Gene Littler and Lee Trevino. (Littler is the man who developed a habit of winning the odd tournament or two early in the year on the US circuit and then, when there seemed enough money in the bank, more or less retiring for the rest of the year to devote himself to the care of his fleet of vintage cars.) However, Gene was still playing in the autumn of 1969 and with Trevino was good enough to beat the British pair by the narrow margin of one hole.

There followed Peter's farewell to Ryder Cup golf and his opponent was a name worthy of the occasion, Lee Trevino. Alliss played finely, though troubled, he says, by the dreaded putting twitches, being out in 34 and two under par at the end of it all. But Trevino was six below and won by two and one.

Though Peter had gained only half a point from his three matches his scoring had rivalled any player's on either side. In the 53 holes he played he had only four times strayed above par and had 15 times been under. Appropriately, the last hole he was to play in the Ryder Cup was a birdie.

Peter did not play in the dramatic final series of singles in the afternoon. Because of his poor putting he asked the captain, Eric Brown, to drop him. Peter also felt that there were young hopefuls who deserved a chance, while his own active career as a full-time tournament golfer was nearing its end. Peter's horizons had never been narrow and he was increasingly involved in TV work and golf architecture. In fact young British hopefuls have seldom done well in the Ryder Cup. Peter remarks that many are full of bounce and bravado beforehand: 'Bring them all on. They've only got two arms and legs like me.' Alas, at least one such bold spirit has been observed vomiting with stage fright half an hour before teeing-off time and others have been trembling wrecks on the course . . .

It is, Peter thinks, not so much the fear of being beaten that does it but the fear of going down by a humiliating margin. Some have felt it impossible to beat certain US golfers. I remember one who had enormous respect for Sam Snead and fervently hoped that their names would not be paired. They were . . . The greatest of credit then to Brian Barnes for beating the great Nicklaus twice in a day.

This most dramatic of Ryder Cups, which ended in a tie with Jack Nicklaus conceding Tony Jacklin a not-so-short putt on the last green in the last match, was Peter's final one.

No one's Ryder Cup record can be assessed merely on a totting up of points scored, because of the three different forms of matchplay used. If X lost his foursomes match in, say, 1937, was this because he played poorly or did Y hit every other tee shot in a troublesome direction and find the hole a four and a half inches diameter geometric figure into which a sphere of roughly one and a half inches diameter resolutely would not fit?

Similarly four-balls, surely both the most social and bastard form of matchplay golf. I suspect the popularity derives from the fact that the reactions to the result from each participant are comforting ones: 'We won,' or 'I didn't lose'. If it's 'We won', Mr X, playing with Mr Y is probably – no, certainly – feeling that he had played his normal game, a combination of considerable power and precision, and had a partner around to exchange the odd word with, though of course the fellow had no real influence on the result. If, however, the result in terms of mere statistics seems to have worked out as a loss, the scope for explanation and excuse is broad indeed. Concentrating on one's own team, one can feel and say (if only to oneself) 'We should have won easily but I had to carry my partner all the way round'. And then the opposition. Apart from the unbelievable number of strokes of fate that favoured them, there was the unkindest one of all. They happened to 'fit in'. On each and every hole one or other of them had been manfully getting his socks wet wading for his ball or disregarding the assaults of brambles upon his person. But while such events were going on, the other was safely plodding up the fairway and dependably getting his putts into the hole. Neither was round in fewer than about 90 but, such is fate, the partnership score was a useful bit better than level par.

In Peter's case then, it is probably fairest to say that over the years only Eric Brown has a better singles record.

Peter's future contribution to these Ryder Cup encounters may eventually be as captain. Certainly he has ideas on what is wrong with the British approach and what can be done to set things more nearly right.

What is most lacking of all is *confidence*. Peter believes that no British team has a real chance on US soil but that no US team should be allowed to win in Britain. Consider US performances in the British Open for instance. True, one of them usually wins it and there will very likely be a couple more in the first five places but a considerable number of major US golfers finish very well down the field or even fail to qualify after the first 36 holes. This is because they have failed to adapt to British conditions. Think of Gene Littler, for instance. For 20 years or so he has been in the very top flight of US golfers, with a swing that has lasted unblemished through the years, but his play in the Open is not worth even a footnote in the history of golf.

Every British player then should feel that on his home ground at least he is the equal of the best US golfers. Once confidence has got that far all might then follow, even in America.

Peter would like to pick the team himself, rather than relying on one of the many systems followed in the past; get them together well before the event; and build up self esteem so that each really believes that his opposite number just has 'two arms and two legs . . .'.

Certainly no previous system of selection has apparently worked any too well. There was one in which a player who had performed well the *previous* season might earn enough points to ensure selection even though his game might then fall to the depths. In a more recent system, Eamonn Darcy more or less ensured his team place by finishing high in just *one* tournament, for that perform-ance happened to be worth a great deal of money and cash won was the basis of selection. One supremo as selector might well work better than this.

Three for immortality

Most of this book has been concerned with greatness of one kind or another in golf. For the final chapter, Peter and I wanted to get away from what is basically the theme of mastery in striking a golf ball. So we have taken three figures from widely-different eras who have become a part of golf legend: Walter Hagen, *the* personality of them all; Young Tom Morris, the first golfer to dominate his own time; and 'Babe' Zaharias, supreme woman athlete of her time who happened to try her hand at the game of golf and added a dimension to women's play.

What? Miss a putt for $2,000? Not likely!

We all have favourite remarks that have been made about golf over the century or more that the game has been popular. Of all I have read and heard, this is the remark with the strongest appeal for me.

Consider the implications. All golfers know full well that the knees are more apt to tremble and the fingers to grip the putter that much too firmly (alas often in a stranglehold) if the putt is in some way or other an 'important' one. It may be a net 66 that is at stake in a monthly medal; one's name inscribed on a cup; a four-footer to get into the hole on the last green to half a four-ball; or 'this one for the Open'. Nearly everyone still remembers how Doug Sanders did not cope with that particular situation any too well at St Andrews in 1970 – no doubt Doug more so than anyone else – but all golfers, though more accustomed to dwelling at great length on moments of triumph, have similar experiences to share with Mr Sanders. I can remember an occasion when I easily missed a putt of no more than six inches to get a half in a four-ball. It wasn't nerves that did it. No, I was unable to concentrate on the minute task in front of me: I was too irritated at the triviality of it, was unwilling to be seen to take pains with it. The result? Well, it went something like this. First the surprised lift of the eyebrows, followed quickly by the devil-may-care grin and then the quick – utterly relaxed of course – step up to the ball. And finally a nice smooth stroke at it that missed the hole by a clear four inches.

Well it was, of course, vanity that found me out. It doesn't seem to with even the most average of professionals of today. Few, if any, are ashamed to take the greatest of pains over their preparations to get a short one safely to bed in the hole. We should not, however, be too impressed by their attention to the details of walking this way and that and lying down here and there and all those tests to see if the hands are still attached to the wrists and the whole human outfit capable of moving a putter back a few inches and then forward again in a more-or-less straight line. No, what they are doing is anything they can think of to delay the frightening moment when they are going to have to give that golf ball a little tap and that all about them may fall down laughing if the result – such as missing the putt – is absurd. They, and we, are in fact more concerned with not making a mess of it than success – and fear destroys.

Which brings me back to our title and to Mr Walter Hagen. His attitude, as put so clearly in the quote, was the reverse of those I've been describing. If there was a putt worth money, he was confident he would not miss it. The incentives for doing it right were what counted for him, not the ignominy of failure.

Confidence was the essence of Walter Hagen the man, and Walter Hagen the golfer. For nearly two decades, he *knew* he could do what was required: hole the putt; play the recovery shot onto the green from forest depths; win an Open; and, above all, beat anyone in matchplay.

He was first heard of on the world scene in September 1913 when he turned up at Brookline Country Club in the US to help his none-too-confident fellow American professionals confront the challenge of Ted Ray and Harry Vardon who were on an exhibition tour of the country and felt they might as well round things off by winning the US Open. Golf has two fairy tales far too impossible to be dreamed up by anyone. One is the playoff victory of Jack

Fleck over Ben Hogan for the 1955 US Open and the other, of course, is Francis Ouimet's similar performance more than 60 years ago at Brookline. Yet Walter Hagen's, rather than Francis's name could have been the one to cause the golf world to reel and become instant legend.

Even more an unknown than Francis Quimet, he kept up a running fight with the invincible Britons and in the end finished three shots behind them. Walter had to bide his time a little but he had made a mark the first time he entered a national championship. After the First World War had ended, there was not to be another championship in Britain or America for many a year in which his name did not figure at the centre of things.

Together with Bobby Jones, Hagen dominated an era. Yet both as golfers and as human beings no pair could have been less alike. Jones as golfer is discussed elsewhere but, in brief, he was a master more of the longer, swinging shots: drive, full irons, and even long putts come into this category – why? Well consider Sam Snead, forced first to putt croquet-style between his legs and, when they banned that, he adopted its nearest equivalent, the so-called 'sidewinder' method. All this because he was twitching the little ones. Sam had few fears on his approach putts.

So what of Walter Hagen as a golf technician? On full shots you could say that he swayed back and lurched forwards and such pronounced body movement led to inconsistency. Perhaps he hit more bad long shots than any golfer of the highest class either before or since his time. On the other hand, as practice makes perfect, Walter spent a good deal of his time amongst the trees, in far-flung parts of the rough and bunkers and from these perilous places struck more miraculous recoveries than anyone else is credited with.

And he knew consummately how to make the best drama out of his miracles. If Walter was in the trees, but had a simple-enough shot to play towards a green, he did not merely walk to his ball and knock it onto the green. On the contrary, the actor took over at this point and the drama began. He would walk out to the fairway, patrol around in the undergrowth, take up as much time as possible before the ball duly came out. He had that feeling for drama (not to mention publicity) that enabled him to get the paying customers involved in the performance.

But Walter was not a player with great power and never employed the strength of a Palmer, for instance, in these feats. If his ball had a bush in the way, Walter was not the man to thrash his way through it.

No, the true talent of the man became apparent when delicacy of touch was the prime requirement. Walter would be the man you would ask to play your shots for you from 100 yards in, chip it to the flag from a fluffy lie or get it near from a bunker. Bunker shots indeed showed Walter at his best. The broad-soled sand wedge has made the explosion shot from consistent sand within the range of any competent club golfer. You just take aim at a point an inch or two behind the ball and hit sand and ball onto the green. But Walter's era came before the sand wedge had either been invented or legalized. He had either to attempt his kind of explosion shot with a thin-edged niblick or, and this was where he was supreme, flick the thing off the surface cleanly. As all golfers know, this is a shot that must be struck exactly. If you take a small spoonful of sand before the ball, the result is that either you remain in the bunker or at best the shot travels nowhere near as far as you intended. Or the reverse is that you stroke it with the leading edge and the ball either thumps dully into the face of the bunker or, perhaps even worse, bores low and long into the rather-too-far distance. And then you have to try to do it better next time from another bunker or try to hit a full wedge, or the like, all the way back again towards the green.

But Walter had probably deftly flicked it onto the green and none too far from the hole. And the putting surface was even more the stage for his talents than were the forests. Quite simply, he was a great sinker of the short and the medium-length putt, and not far behind at getting the long ones close.

During the 1920s it was long disputed who was the better all-round golfer, Jones or Hagen. No one else really came into it except, just possibly, Gene Sarazen. Miller and Nicklaus today fight shy of playing in matchplay because of the instant damage defeat would do to their reputation. No one thinks much the worse of a man for not winning an open or run-of-the-mill tournament but if you lose a match, you have most definitely been beaten for the whole world to see.

So Jones had his selection of championships won and so did

Hagen. It was better for both, especially Hagen with a living to earn as a professional, not to risk the damage to reputation of being beaten in man-to-man combat.

But eventually, more than 50 years ago, they met over 72 holes in February and March 1926. At this point in time, Hagen had been beaten but four times in matchplay.

Hagen immediately went into the lead. Short in two on the first hole, he ran it up to not much more than a foot. Jones, through the back in two with a chip to play along a downslope, was less successful and his ball ran several yards past. Although, from that point on, the first round was closely fought and holes were exchanged, Hagen's putter was more magical than Jones's. Bobby used only 31 putts but Hagen had just 27. When they went off to lunch, Walter was three up.

For the first nine holes in the afternoon, the position remained much the same. A crucial event took place on the 6th. Both drove well and Jones sent his second shot onto the green while Walter contemplated the problem of having pine trees between him and the green. His mind made up about the kind of shot he would have to play, Walter then proceeded to hit a bad one – half topped and sliced. But the unwholesome thing ran along the ground quite nicely, then through a bunker, then up a bank and in the end it lay only a few feet from the hole. A three for Walter, four for Jones.

With nine holes of the day remaining, Walter decided that as he was now three up he could hardly finish the first 36 holes of the match in too disastrous a position. On the other hand, by attacking play he might build an unassailable lead. Walter attacked. Bold shots came off. He was back in 32 and Jones was eight down for the second 36 holes a week later in Pasadena. Although Jones had used 30 putts only, which is good going, Hagen had four fewer.

Putting counted equally a week later. Jones had to make immediate inroads into the Hagen lead. After halving the 1st, both were a long way from the hole on the 2nd. Bobby putted his up dead; Hagen sank his. Nine up.

A couple of holes later Bobby was himself favoured by fortune: he chipped in. But Walter cancelled it out by holing a long putt. With 12 holes to go Walter had the comforting thought that he could not be beaten for he was 12 up. But Bobby Jones was not quite dead. On the next hole he again chipped in for a birdie. But Hagen's chip also went down.

Game set and match to Hagen and $7,500 as well, a lot of money in 1926 and not to be spurned even today.

But the experience did Bobby no lasting damage it seems; he accomplished the rare feat of winning both the British and US Opens not very much later that very same year . . .

Things of this sort did not always go so well for Walter even though in temperament he was unexcelled as a match player. In 1928 he decided to make a foray to Britain for the Open. To help pay expenses a challenge match was an attractive idea. Archie Compston, at this time probably the best British golfer, was selected as opponent and Moor Park was chosen as the venue. Walter, though there was money to be won, can hardly have been taking the match seriously.

The Atlantic, of course, was crossed by liner in those days and a luxurious process that was. Especially for Walter, who was apt to run up a liquor bill of formidable proportions. He arrived on 25 April and the 72-hole match began less than two days later. Hagen was out of touch and unfit. The match was virtually over in fact after just half a round.

Compston won four of the first six holes and was out in 32 to Hagen's 38 to be five up. He then followed with a two on the 10th and, though 72 holes is a long journey, to be six down with 62 to go is not an encouraging prospect. Nevertheless Walter now began to make something of a fight back. He held his own the rest of the way back to the clubhouse and went into lunch 'only' four down after taking the 18th.

People were beginning to wonder if Walter hadn't deliberately been taking things a bit easily to make quite sure that there'd be a match still alive for the final 18 holes the following afternoon. Well the match was still alive but not in quite the way you'd have expected.

That first afternoon, the holes once again began to slip away from Hagen so that he was seven down after 27 holes had been played. Landslide followed as Compston produced one of the greatest purple patches of his career: he came back in 30 and won no fewer than seven of the holes played on that second half. At the end of the afternoon Compston had gone round in 66, Hagen in 76. Compston had putted steadily, particularly in his holing out, whereas Walter claimed he had three-putted five times – most unHagenlike behaviour. Anyway, back to his London hotel 14 down. See you tomorrow morning Archie . . .

On the 18th the next day Hagen found that he had to hole a putt of several yards to keep the match alive, and get the paying customers in, for the final afternoon round. He did so and went to lunch dormie 18 down.

There has never in golf history that I know of been a recovery from anything like that position and this paragraph has no fairy-tale ending. Walter halved the 1st hole in the afternoon and that was that.

Hagen realized that something drastic would have to be done with both his form and his high-living habits. As a concession to this regrettable necessity he abandoned liquor, women and late nights for *several* days and substituted a diet of golf, Turkish baths, plain cooking and early to bed.

He then won the 1928 Open Championship.

Even so, the Compston match may have been a sign that at long last the writing was on the wall. Fifteen years at the top is longer than all but a select few have survived. Think of Palmer and Hogan, for example. Both won all their major championships in the space of half-a-dozen years. But Walter had one, perhaps his greatest, achievement before him.

For British golfers, competing on the opposite side of the Atlantic was both expensive and unusual. Very few British golfers, for instance, tried their luck in America during the 1920s. Peter Alliss recalls that his father Percy decided to attempt the Canadian Open in 1931. The journey from his club job in Berlin to Toronto took three weeks. He probably felt it was worthwhile for he tied for first place and did not lose the playoff till the 38th hole. The winner? Walter Hagen . . .

Hagen again came over the British Open the following year, which was held at Muirfield, one of the most formidable tests of golf in the world and especially so if the winds blow. And they did.

For the first two days of the qualifying rounds they were at near-gale force with lashing rain. When the Championship proper began on the Wednesday a total of 162 was good enough to qualify.

Hagen was comfortably in with 154 but he was not the favourite. These were Macdonald Smith, Horton Smith and the brilliant but flawed Leo Diegel. This last was something of a believer in gimmicks. Like many another, he experimented both with his putting style and with putters. He brought six with him and decided to use two of them, one for short putts and another for long ones. This is perhaps sensible enough. Haven't we all felt confident at holing the short ones with a particular brand but not at getting the long ones up close? And vice versa? But Leo went further than this. He liked to have a *new* putter in his bag, something that, just possibly, might transform this part of his game. But, alas, he couldn't find a new putter that he liked. There was nothing else for it. He painted the shaft of one he already had. Leo was content. He had something that *looked* new.

And he had another gimmick that most thought far more eccentric. Leo *wore a glove on his left hand*! The man from *The Times* – presumably the great Bernard Darwin – described this as 'very rare', and implied that professionals, or even good golfers, should be above such useless affectations.

I'm an anti-glove man myself. I like Max Faulkner's opinion which is that if your lefthand grip needs artificial aid then so probably does your right, so wear two gloves. To me, though, the main drawback of wearing a glove is that it tends to conceal a faulty or weak grip. If you don't have a glove on there will be the useful reminder of blisters or at least sore places after a round that you are not 'holding on' nearly well enough. This may stimulate thoughts about just what is wrong with your particular grip on the club with your left hand. (Peter Alliss does not agree with these thoughts. He points out that smooth skin and sweat can lead to a club slipping and feels a *good* glove is an essential. He recalls, however, that Hogan, Locke and Thomson of recent great ones did not wear gloves and that neither does Hubert Green.) In the light of all this, what of Henry Cotton? He took to a glove after thumb damage and then discarded 'worn out' ones as often as once a round. Expensive business.

For a while, both glove and painted shaft worked very well for Leo, and so also did his swing, which was also idiosyncratic. He would perch the ball on an exceptionally-high tee and then stand very upright, almost as if he were trying to get himself away from that ball and which, just possibly, he could miss altogether if the clubhead happened to pass clear underneath and send nothing but a tee peg down the fairway. Then came the backswing, performed with a pronounced dip at the knees, which of course had to straighten again as he came into the ball.

Never mind. Eccentric or not Leo covered Muirfield twice that Wednesday and Thursday and at the end of it all stood comfortably in the lead after rounds of 71, 69. This was exceptional scoring on a course that was playing very long, but with very fast greens. As well as playing long, it *was* long. About 6,700 yards in fact which in effect, if not yardage, is far longer than any championship course of today. Remember, they might have long been using the Haskell ball-making principle but one must at least believe the present-day manufacturers' advertisement claims to the extent of agreeing that, yes, a 1970s ball does go further than one made 50 years ago. And there is no doubt at all that it is far easier to hit full out with a steel shaft than to cope with the torsion of a hickory one. The main result of all this was that if you were, for example, playing a long par four and hit a superb drive, you still expected to be playing a long iron for your second shot, not a nudge with a 9 iron.

Yet Leo, though he led at this point, had not been outshining everyone. Percy Alliss, for example, of whom at the time it was said, 'No one of the British players has a truer, sweeter, simpler swing', did a 69 and that was the first time that anyone had broken 70 at Muirfield. Not surprisingly it gave him the first round lead and though he had 76 next time out he was still well in the hunt. Perhaps the putting had gone once again. Peter recalls his father talking about another memorable Open, Sarazen's 1932 win, and remarking that if he had just managed to get the ball into the hole in two putts 72 times he would have won by several shots.

And what of our hero?

He began with a 75 which it might be fair to call the sort of score that didn't at all put you out of it but . . . Well, do not do it too often.

This, against the Muirfield card that May of 1929 (never mind the par, Muirfield is one of the very few courses that refuses to allow a par to a hole) is what Walter did after breakfast on Thursday:

1	450	4	
2	353	4	
3	380	3	
4	180	3	
5	510	4	
6	450	3	
7	153	3	
8	455	5	
9	483	4	33 out
10	459	4	
11	359	4	
12	380	4	
13	128	3	
14	400	3	
15	393	4	
16	193	3	
17	507	5	
18	410	4	34 in

67

Obviously it was a course record, eclipsing Alliss's round of the previous day, but remember this in the context that Muirfield had not, before this Championship, ever been covered in fewer than 70 strokes.

The none-too-modest Walter Hagen thought it perhaps the best round he had ever played, one of those rare occasions that the pursuit of Dame Golf may eventually offer us. Suddenly we are no longer aware of any problem in striking the ball both precisely and rather hard: the whole process feels as natural and unforced as aiming a fork at the dead centre of the mouth and then precisely and firmly teeth and lips close inexorably upon that nugget of steak. No problem at all. And of course much the same kind of thing as regards the putting. You, and that day Walter, just give a glance at the correct route to the hole and tap the ball at the right pace towards it and, naturally, in it goes.

But let us pause for a moment and look again at that card of Walter's for really in the 1920s it was comfortably the best round played in a major championship. The outstanding feature of it is how well he played the long par fours: 1, 6, 8, 10, 14, 18. True there was the flaw of a shot dropped on the 8th but a couple of birdies too to make up for it.

Jones's 1926 Sunningdale round of 66 is even more legendary but this was in a qualifying round for the British Open of that year. Was it more perfect? Possibly, for Jones sank but one putt of any length and the ultimate test of a round of golf is usually thought to be hitting all the fairways and all the greens with putting a less-admired but, unfortunately necessary, after event.

In fact, few details have come down to us of the hole-by-hole play of Hagen's round because it was an inevitable part, and still is, of the golf reporter's life that he is always at point B when it is all happening at point A. Or watching X because he is the man in form and will surely soon stop stroking it fluently into the rough and three-putting? Whereas it is Y who is actually in the process of winning the Masters or the US Open or whatever. Today, of course, there are a large number of TV cameras looming overhead and hand-held below, and if they do not see anything then the man of the day is always available for detailed interview and can be relied on to remember what happened an hour or two before.

The Hagen round did not in fact begin at all perfectly. At the 1st, he missed the green and was bunkered, but there followed a clean flick from the sand and the ball nearly went in the hole. Tap in for a four. On the 2nd, Hagen pushed his drive out to the right and then missed the green with his second shot. His third go at it also did not much improve matters: he was still an uncomfortable number of yards from the hole. But the putt went straight into the middle and that was probably the end of self questioning for Walter. True, his second shot to the 8th was not hit quite decisively enough, and it kicked unkindly into a bunker. It was the only hole at which he strayed over par.

Yet it did not give him the outright lead. He lay two shots behind Leo Diegel but Leo was far more likely to disappear from sight than a Hagen with the bit between his teeth. So it proved. The next day Leo had an 82 and that sounded almost as bad in 1929 as it would today.

So one day of play – and 36 holes – remained. Throughout, there were squalls of rain and a consistent near gale from the south west. Before play began, Hagen said that a couple of 75s would win the Championship for anybody in the leading group. He was right. And he had brought with him one particular tool of his trade that helped him substantially to be the man to do two 75s: a bullet-headed driver. This was a club with both a deep and a straight face and it had but one function: to hit the ball low under the full force of the wind. It is said that his drives never rose higher than 20 feet.

He began his third round 4, 4, 4, 3, 4, 4, solid indeed in the conditions, and reached the turn in 37, whereas Leo Diegel was almost gone after a 43 out. As the white horses rose on the Firth of Forth, Walter continued apparently quite composed on his way, now playing the stretch of course most lengthened by the wind. At lunchtime, he had the first of those 75s. Today it may sound something like four over par but it was the 75, not his 67 the day before, that set him firmly in the lead. Amongst those in contention, none bettered it and not a few would have been happy to equal it.

After three rounds, this was the position:

217	Hagen
221	Alliss
222	Mitchell
222	Diegel
223	Farrell

In the afternoon, perhaps the conditions were just slightly easier, for certainly the scoring was the odd stroke better. One player in fact did better 75 by a single shot. That was the expatriate Cornish-man, Jim Barnes, but he was far out of the running. Otherwise no one made up ground on Walter and nearly all went even further behind.

Hagen made sure of it all in the first half. After seven holes he had used only 26 shots and then came to the 8th, where he had 'spoiled' that perfect round the previous day. He had been thinking about this hole. It was laid out as a dogleg to the right with deep rough at the angle. But this rough had been trampled flat by the spectators. Walter decided to push his drive into it, intending to shorten his shot into the green at this 455-yard hole. The drive went where he wanted it to and he followed with a pitch to a couple of yards and a single putt. The Muirfield authorities are not to be mocked. Afterwards they planted buckthorn and today the hole *has* to be played as a dogleg. Not surprisingly, though, it is known as 'Hagen's Hole'. But after this piece of cheek Walter immediately lost some of the ground he had gained by taking six on the 483-yard 9th. He had hooked one hard up against a wall but produced a lefthanded club from his cavernous bag (Hagen's bag was always bigger than anyone else's and his caddies better paid) and put it on the front edge of the green.

So he was out in 35 and the Championship his, provided he could coast home avoiding disaster. There was, as history knows, no disaster and in fact he played one particular hole, the 14th, 'only' 400 yards but it was taking three woods to reach it, better than anyone else for a par four. In the event, he was back in 40 having nonchalantly missed a putt of little more than a yard on the last. So that was Walter's second 75.

This is how he, and the rest of them, finished:

292 Hagen
298 Farrell
299 Diegel
300 Mitchell, Alliss
301 Cruikshank
303 Barnes
304 Watrous, Sarazen
305 Armour

Anglophiles were distressed to note that from this listing above of ten names, eight of them were Americans. There were post mortems held to view the corpse of British golf and to decide whether or not there were any ways by which it might be revived at some point in the future, a debate that continues (like that over the British economy) to this day. But no one minded that Walter had won it. Hagen and Jones victories were always popular for both, in the public mind, seemed to rest on some pinnacle above mere nationalism. It might rankle that too many Americans had finished ahead of far too many Britons but Hagen and Jones were the acknowledged inheritors of the mantles of Taylor, Braid, Ray and Vardon. It was right and proper that one of them should win.

The British Press of the day were apt to spend lead in discussing the chances of George Duncan, Abe Mitchell, Archie Compston and Percy Alliss but more as a gesture than a matter of conviction.

With this Hagen victory, followed a year later by Bobby Jones's total dominance, golf came to the end of an era. Jones retired, Hagen ceased to be a winner of major championships. His swing improved, the sway and lurch noticeably lessened and it was remarked that Walter was not seen in wild country as often as before. But as the full shots grew more controlled, the deft flicks from sand and the hand on the putter both became less sure. Walter continued to win tournaments from time to time but at Muirfield in 1929 he had reached a peak at which his long game was more sure than ever before and he could still stand, legs splayed, rock steady in the bluster of the wind and, unaffected, stroke the ball into the middle of the hole.

The first of a few

Wherever sports lovers gather, the chat very often gets around to the theme of 'Who was the greatest of them all?'. How, for example, does Paavo Nurmi compare with Lasse Viren, Jesse Owens with Borzov, Jack Hobbs or Victor Trumper with Don Bradman or Barry Richards, Tilden and Laver, Juan Fangio and Jim Clark . . .

The questions can never be decided because the yardsticks for judging men and women of different eras just do not exist. Obviously it is impossible to prove that Barry Richards is a greater attacking batsman than a Trumper, Charles Macartney or a Gilbert Jessop but the same holds true even of athletic events for which recorded times and measurements are usually available. In this case it must, on the face of it, seem that Jim Montgomery is a better sprint swimmer than Johnny Weismuller, because in the 1976 Olympic Games he swam the 100 metres freestyle in fewer than 50 seconds whereas Weismuller was content to win by breaking the one-minute barrier. Perhaps that last phrase is the key. Human beings have an inbuilt target and that target is usually associated with *winning* more than anything else. You do what is necessary to win and not too much more. Of course there are exceptions, the most notable perhaps being Bob Beamon's world and Olympic long-jump record which looks as if it may stand for ever. But perhaps the long jump is a very special event in sport. When competing you are basically concerned with trying to hurl yourself through space as far as you possibly can. Beamon, a variable sort of performer, happened to get the hurling exactly right for those few moments in time, irrespective of the quality of the opposition.

But in golf, the opposition always remains in mind even though a golfer may also be thinking of playing the unattainable perfect round. This, in essence, consists of hitting a very long drive straight down a fairway, followed by an iron shot very close indeed to the hole (we will have to allow that hitting those particular shots straight down the hole are made impossible by subtle shifts in the wind strength and direction as a golf ball flies through the air, and the actual condition of each square centimetre of turf on a green, and this the golfer cannot perceive from afar). Then, of course, your golfer in hot pursuit of the ideal knocks each and every one of those short putts into the middle of the hole. So his total for the round will be in the region of 50 (naturally, he reaches all the par fives in two strokes). But in competition no golfer, however much he may talk about 'playing the course', forgets that there are a lot of other golfers out there and his aim is to get, and stay, ahead of them. To win is of the essence, how many you took does go down in the record books but that is just about all.

As winners then in their various eras Nicklaus, Player, Palmer, Hogan, Snead and, above all, Jones, were supreme and the argument usually concentrates on these, sometimes with Joyce Wethered thrown in for good measure. Yet if we go back much further in time we come eventually, via Vardon, Taylor and Braid, to the name of Young Tom Morris, a man who lorded it over his contemporaries more thoroughly and inevitably than any since. 'But,' you may say, 'the opposition wasn't up to much.' This is a statement made of every era right up to the present day when the swing of a Nicklaus, Palmer or Miller still remains on the retina. Certainly the number of likely winners of an open championship in Morris's day were a handful only, and the competitors reckoned in dozens not hundreds.

Tom was born in 1851, the son of a man who was to win the Open in 1861 and repeat that feat three times more. There is no record of when Young Tom (so called to distinguish him from Old Tom, his father) first began to play golf but no doubt it was as early as most who have a golfing father. But by the time he was 13 his fame had spread sufficiently for prize money of five pounds to be put up for a match between him and another young hopeful. The match was followed by 'hundreds of deeply interested and anxious spectators'. A far cry perhaps from the 20,000 plus who watch a British or American open but this was an quarter of a century *before* a handful only of spectators watched Vardon win his first Open.

You would not have expected much of a discourse on technique from an observer of the match and what has come down to us emphasizes mainly the neatness of his swing and his accuracy. Young Tom was to develop other qualities in his short career.

Three years later Young Tom won his first tournament. Held at Carnoustie, this was played over 30 holes for 'prizes to the value of twenty pounds'. Thirty-two were entered and Tom, at 16, tied for first place with two others and then won the playoff comfortably. Next came his first entry in an open championship. His father won and Young Tom finished in fourth place, five strokes behind.

An average length for a golf course today is about 6,150 yards, while those used for championships and most tournaments will be in the region of 7,000. Whatever their length they 'naturally' have 18 holes. 'But why 18?', you may now well ask, if you haven't done so before. And the answer is that St Andrews happened to have a stretch of linksland over which people have knocked a ball from time immemorial and with the passing of time it became the custom to start off from various point A's and finish with holes at various point B's. The total that the stretch of linksland turned out to accommodate was 18 holes. In due course every club felt that it had to provide 18 also but at the Carnoustie of 1867 ten holes had evolved and I'm sure no one in the very least felt that there ought to be 18. Probably nearly every golf course in the world would be a finer one if the land available had been used to the best advantage for eight holes, 14, 19 or whatever the landscape happened to suggest. But there we are, 18 it has to be because of the precedent set by St Andrews, home of golf. The result inevitably is that a clear majority of courses must average four dull holes that had to be slotted in amongst those of finer quality in order to make up the mandatory 18. This will never change now, for golfers at every level have become far too used to saying they have shot a 66, broken 80 or whatever . . .

The next year Young Tom beat his father for the Championship, winning by three shots with the score of 157. Prestwick was where the Open was always played at that time over a 12-hole course. These were the yardages of the day with an estimate of par and Young Tom's score for each during his first round:

		Par?	Tom Morris
1	578	6	6
2	385	5	4
3	167	3	4
4	448	5	6
5	440	5	5
6	314	4	5
7	144	3	3
8	166	3	1
9	395	5	6
10	213	4	3
11	132	3	3
12	417	5	4
		51	50

'What?', you say, 'only one under par?'. But consider that the Prestwick of 1868 – and for a good many years thereafter – was a stretch of linksland that had been allowed to remain much as nature had designed, that golf was basically a game in which you started off from one point and finished at another and that you then took a few paces and teed up your ball again. Of course, I have not mentioned 'greens' or 'fairways' because these did not exist. In fact, you no doubt often found yourself putting over the very patch of ground from which you would next be hitting a tee shot. What a putting surface was like is very clearly demonstrated by a comment of the early golf writer H.S.C. Everard, writing of Young Tom's choice of putting implements a couple of decades later. 'He invariably used a putter; curiously enough, he was quite unable to use a cleek (similar to a 1 iron of today but with a narrower face) for a *bad-lying putt*; (my italics) these he negotiated with his iron, which was very straight in the face.'

These remarks show clearly that while some areas of a putting surface might happen to be fairly smooth, the average was nearer to a fairway of today – in poor condition.

For play through the green Tom would have had, literally, a handful of clubs, all shafted with hickory and matched only to the extent that he had chosen clubs of similar feel. If indeed you have from time to time seen the odd club of extreme age remember that these almost certainly date from much later in the nineteenth century when club-making skills had been refined by longer experience. Tom's clubs would have been far more clumsy. And he was hitting a ball made of gutta percha for which 180 yards would have been a good hit.

At Prestwick the following year Young Tom put together rounds of 51, 54, 49 – good enough for victory by 11 strokes, while his third round of 49 set a new record.

The next year he did a little better, eclipsing his closest pursuer by 12 strokes, with a total of 149 which had still not been bettered when eventually the event was played over 72 holes from 1892 onwards.

During the 1870 Open Young Tom had one round of 47, four under a par that was thought of as impossible perfection. He must have been encouraged by his playing of the 1st hole – 570 yards – which he did in three. There were no witnesses but it must have gone: drive, another drive, and then yet another straight into the hole. Thereafter he strayed above par but once.

With this third win, Young Tom had created a problem: he had won the red-leather, silver-mounted belt which was competed for each year outright. As a result, no Championship was held in the following year, 1871.

By 1872, the decision had been taken to award the trophy which is still competed for today. Of course, Young Tom won it. In the same year he also set a course record for St Andrews that stood for many years when he went round the 18-hole course in 77. This broke the previous best by two strokes at a time when something in the region of 87 was the score that the best of the day expected to achieve over the links. Indeed the previous record had been a kind of fluke set up in the course of a private match.

Young Tom was now nearing the end of both his golfing career and his life. There seems to have been some falling off in form and he may well have begun to suffer from consumption.

His story ends with the sad tale of how he was playing with his father in a challenge match at what is now the West Course at North Berwick against the Park brothers, for £25 a side. The Morrises won and a telegram then arrived stating that Young Tom's wife was dangerously ill. Father and son were loaned a sailing boat and put out from North Berwick harbour. When they arrived, his wife was dead.

Young Tom followed only three months later.

But what, then, were his qualities as a golfer? The qualities that his contemporaries singled out were remarkably similar to what we would expect of an open champion of today. He was, for example, the first of the great putters, able to hole nearly all the short ones and lay the longer ones dead this (as already mentioned) over rough patches of turf, and it is said that, Nicklaus like, he took a great deal of time over the short ones. In driving, he sounds to have a similar method to Palmer – not too long a backswing and then everything flung at the ball. Again like Palmer, and Ben Hogan, all his shots were flighted low, and this made him a more competitive player the more the wind blew. Little more is known of him except that all were amazed at his powers of recovery from bad lies, but perhaps this is enough : like nearly all the Great Ones we can see that he was the best putter of his day, developed full power from a three-quarter swing and could deal with what trouble he found. That's a recipe that has tended to produce an open champion in most decades of the last hundred years or so.

Athlete as golfer

I once knew a butcher who tossed sides of beef here and there with easy disdain. He was, it soon came out, a keen golfer and a game was arranged. As I had expected, so powerful a man was a very fair golfer but not at all in the ways I anticipated. The man was a very good putter, read each green to a nicety and stroked the ball precisely up to the hole and, very often, into it. He was similarly deft in chipping the ball up dead with a 6 or 7 iron. From the tee it was exceptional for him not to be very near the middle of the fairway.

His handicap was 15. Why no fewer than this barely respectable status? Well, this broad-shouldered, iron-forearmed, steely-wristed Colossus just couldn't move a golf ball any distance at all. The clubhead did not accelerate. There would be a slow measured, even rhythmic, backswing and the process was much the same on the downswing. At no point was there any snap whatsoever in the performance. The 15 handicap resulted because it is very difficult to score better than this if your best shot carries about 100 yards and rolls on another 50 – if the ground is hard.

This absence of snap in the swing is one of the main shortcomings in the makeup of the majority of women golfers. There is the long backswing, and then the downswing and attack on the ball are accomplished without notable increase in momentum. Surprisingly, perhaps, this applies to the game around the green as well – the chips and short pitches.

Of course there are exceptions and possibly the most notable of all was a woman who was an athlete first and then, much later, a championship golfer: Mildred Ella Didrickson, usually known as 'the Babe'.

Babe Didrickson was born in 1914 and first gave proof of her games-playing ability by selection for the All-America basketball team in 1930 and 1931. As an athlete she won no less than eight national titles in track and field between 1930 and 1932, a year in which she won five events in the US Amateur Athletic Union championships, tied for first in another and also had a fourth place to her credit.

Two weeks or so later came the 1932 Olympics at Los Angeles. The Babe won gold medals in the javelin and 80 metres high hurdles. In the high jump she was disqualified while tied for first place. Nowadays we have the technique for getting over a bar known as the 'Fosbury Flop' after its innovator, a technique that means that there must be a very soft landing area indeed if the jumper is not to break his or her neck and/or fracture the skull for, as all golfing high jumpers know full well, you go over and down head first. The Babe was disqualified for using a far less extreme technique, the Western Roll, when other competitors were using the then normal Straddle. Whatever the rights and wrongs of the case it is clear that Babe Didrickson could run, throw and jump phenomenally well.

How, wondered Grantland Rice, doyen of US sports writers, would these natural abilities translate onto a golf course? The Babe was persuaded to give the game a try and, still during the Olympics, swung a club at a ball for the first time. She found she could hit it more than 200 yards: undoubtedly there was a fair amount of snap in *her* swing.

It was obvious that there were no more worlds for her to conquer in athletics and she began increasingly to turn her efforts to golf, where her progress was by no means as rapid as might have been expected because of the dual nature of the game. A golfer must basically have two natural or learned abilities: be able to swing a club, whether a wedge or driver, at a ball at high speed – that's the athletic part of it – but must equally be able to give the ball a tap here and a nudge there with equal effectiveness. The Babe was soon able to strike a ball fiercely – though not always in the right direction – but the subtleties of chipping and putting she found far less easy to manage.

Early on she watched the great Jones play a round of golf and the sight is said to have inspired her. By 1934 she felt ready to enter a tournament for the first time and performed respectably. The following year, she won her first tournament but was still something of a freak in a way that probably retarded her career in the game: people wanted to see how far she could hit a golf ball, just as you might go to a sideshow at a circus in curiosity about the length of a lady's beard.

The Babe obliged by hitting the thing as hard as she could; true, her game improved but the improvement was not speeded by this circus-act element.

She became a professional and it seemed a good spectacle to someone to arrange a tour in which she was teamed with Sarazen against Horton Smith and the greatest of all women golfers of her time, as perhaps any other, Joyce Wethered. The Babe proved able to hit a long iron about the same distance as Joyce could her driver, but over a round Joyce was apt to score about ten strokes lower. Nevertheless, the contact with these players of the highest class helped the Babe to improve. Sarazen, for instance, can claim to have invented the sand wedge. He had decided early in the 1930s that a club was needed for sand shots that would ride through the sand, rather than dig down into it, and had experimented with building up the back of the sole of the club. The eventual new weapon was a success and he won both the US and British Opens in 1932, partly as a result of his new ability to get the ball out of a bunker and near to the hole.

During the tour, some of his proficiency rubbed off on the Babe and eventually she became an excellent bunker player – particularly useful as her length from the tee, coupled with occasional wildness, meant that she got into quite a few of them.

In 1938 she married George Zaharias, a practitioner of one of the few sports the Babe had not tried, wrestling. She was an excellent figure skater and swimmer and attained a good standard at billiards, baseball, softball and even football. In fact there is little doubt that in the sports and athletics field the Babe could perform more than competently at anything at all she cared to try.

Financial security with her marriage meant that the Babe no longer had to strive to be a long-hitting freak on the golf course and she was able to concentrate on being simply a very good all-round golfer. She decided to play again as an amateur but of course the war took what should have been the peak years of her career from about 26 to 30.

However, in 1946 she won the US Amateur Championship 11 and nine in the final after a succession of easy victories and then went ahead to win a string of other tournaments in a row that year. In 1947 she did even better and had a stretch of 17 consecutive tournament victories.

It was time to prove herself in Britain and on a links course.

The British Women's Championship that year was played at Gullane No. 1, a course just over a hill from Muirfield and scarcely its inferior as a test of golf. Gullane was wet and playing very long. This served to demonstrate the Babe's hitting powers. She played a fair cross section of the leading British women of the day and convincingly beat all those she encountered. Her power off the tee must have daunted the bravest of them. For example, she needed only a wedge to the green at a long uphill par four, misjudging her shot, sent a 4 iron second clear over the back of the green at a par five measuring 540 yards. In the first round she was home by six and five, in the second by four and two, the third six and four and in the fourth by six and five again. In the fifth round she met Miss Frances Stephens, who was later to win the British women's title twice and be runner-up on two other occasions. Frances gave the Babe her closest run in the Championship but even so went down by three and two.

In the semi-final, she met Miss Jean Donald who was to be runner-up the following year. Babe Zaharias was five under level fours when the match ended very far from home.

The final was played over 36 holes against Miss Jacqueline Gordon, who played sturdily and in fact achieved the unprecedented feat of holding a lead : at the 11th she was two up. Both were eventually round in an approximate 75 and at lunch the match was all square.

In the afternoon it was a different story : if anything Mrs Zaharias played even better, while Miss Gordon did not. Perhaps it was all more or less over in the first two holes. Miss Gordon made an error on the 1st and that was one gone, and then to rub home the lesson the Babe eagled the second. The match came to an end with a five and four victory. However, Miss Gordon had done very well to snatch an outright lead at any stage. Prior to that, the Babe had lost only four holes in the course of her matches against six opponents! This alone is evidence of her power. No one ever suggested of her that she always kept the ball on the fairway but once she was bunkered or in the rough she had the power that nearly all women lack to force it not only out but well up the course.

Before and in the earlier days of the Championship Mrs Zaharias had not always pleased either administrators or Public. For a start, she had turned up to play in corduroy trousers and when she was observed on her way to the 1st tee for the final, in Bermuda shorts, she was asked to please return to the lesser of two evils. She had also seemed arrogant, when being interviewed, by claiming that she had beaten each of the US Walker Cup team, playing level. Apocryphal or not, such a feat was almost certainly not beyond her.

So, the Babe was the first American woman to take the British Women's. There was no doubt at all that she could do it again as and when she wished, while exactly the same applied to the US Amateur. But she decided to return to the professional ranks.

The following year she won the US Open and was leading money winner, a position she was to hold for a further three consecutive years. She also won the US Open in 1950 and 1954 and a total of 33 tournaments in what was a relatively short career as a professional. The 1954 win was a particularly meritorious one: she had been operated on for cancer the year before.

But the disease was not to be denied and in 1956 she died at the age of 42.

Was she the greatest of women golfers? With the passing of the years this has come to be more in doubt. Since her time there have been several women who could probably have matched her in length, while Joyce Wethered still has no rival as an exponent of the aesthetics of the golf swing. There is also Catherine Lacoste who won just about every open there was in 1969.

Undoubtedly the Babe had showed others the way: that there was no reason physically for a woman not to be able to hit the ball a long way whereas before it had been accepted that a woman, at best, swept the ball off a tee peg with a rhythmic and decorous swing; after the Babe there seemed no overriding reason why she should not hit it as far as a good-class male golfer.

The Babe had indeed been asked the secret of her power from the tee and had given an answer more indicative of her golf philosophy than her concern to maintain a feminine image: 'I jest take off my girdle and beat it.'

But to me her progress as a golfer illustrates another aspect of the game even more graphically: it takes a long time to learn. The Babe had been a world-class basketball player at the age of 16 and a supreme athlete a couple of years later. And we have seen that as soon as she swung a golf club it was apparent that she had a great talent for the game. Yet her progress to the top was slow: it took her some 15 years to get the hang of the thing. In every golf club you find similar examples, though at a less-exalted level. In this case, it is the man of 45 to 50, who perhaps took up the game in his middle 30s. Only after a decade or so does he quite suddenly make the transition from being a 14 or 15 handicapper to the high plateau of single figures.

The truth of the matter is that in any sport you have to get the striking implement into the correct hitting position, whether it is a golf club, a racquet or even a football boot. Lash furiously as you may, nothing at all satisfactory will happen to the ball unless your implement is lashing in exactly the right direction. Think, for instance, of the violent swirler of a bat in cricket and baseball. Usually, as does the unskilled golfer, they swing *across* the line. A much more modest effort exerted *down* the line will produce a far more impressive result. But the *natural* way of swinging golf club, cricket bat, baseball bat, racquet is *across* the line. Think how much easier you may have found it to hit a cross-court drive or volley in tennis, rather than one straight down the line.

I wonder if my butcher ever managed it? I know he'd have been delighted, as James Braid is said to have done, to wake up one morning and find himself a long hitter. But I expect John has still to be content with lack of snap and is just sweeping them along the middle and needing to get down in one putt for his par.

Tournament Records

THE OPEN CHAMPIONSHIP

The Belt

Year	Winner	Venue	Score
1860	W. Park	Musselburgh	174
1861	T. Morris, Sen.	Prestwick	163
1862	T. Morris, Sen.	Prestwick	163
1863	W. Park	Musselburgh	168
1864	T. Morris, Sen.	Prestwick	167
1865	A. Strath	St Andrews	162
1866	W. Park	Musselburgh	169
1867	T. Morris, Sen.	St Andrews	170
1868	T. Morris, Jun.	St Andrews	157
1869	T. Morris, Jun.	St Andrews	154
1870	T. Morris, Jun.	St Andrews	149

Tom Morris Jun. was allowed to keep the Belt after he had won it for the third successive year. The Championship was not held in 1871. The following year the present cup was awarded for annual competition.

The Cup

Year	Winner	Venue	Score
1872	T. Morris, Jun.	St Andrews	166
1873	T. Kidd	St Andrews	179
1874	M. Park	Musselburgh	159
1875	W. Park	Musselburgh	166
1876	B. Martin	St Andrews	176
1877	J. Anderson	Musselburgh	160
1878	J. Anderson	Prestwick	157
1879	J. Anderson	St Andrews	170
1880	B. Ferguson	Musselburgh	162
1881	B. Ferguson	Prestwick	170
1882	B. Ferguson	St Andrews	171
1883	W. Fernie	Musselburgh	159
1884	J. Simpson	Carnoustie	160
1885	B. Martin	St Andrews	171
1886	D. Brown	Musselburgh	157
1887	W. Park, Jun.	Prestwick	161
1888	J. Burns	Musselburgh	171
1889	W. Park, Jun.	Musselburgh	155
1890	Mr J. Ball	Royal Liverpool	164
1891	H. Kirkaldy	St Andrews	166

After 1891 the competition was extended to seventy-two holes and for the first time entry money was imposed.

Year	Winner		Venue	Score
1892	Mr H.H. Hilton	Royal Liverpool	Muirfield	305
1893	W. Auchterlonie	St Andrews	Prestwick	322
1894	J.H. Taylor	Winchester	Sandwich	326
1895	J.H. Taylor	Winchester	St Andrews	322
1896	H. Vardon	Ganton	Muirfield	316
1897	Mr H.H. Hilton	Royal Liverpool	Hoylake	314
1898	H. Vardon	Ganton	Prestwick	307
1899	H. Vardon	Ganton	Sandwich	310
1900	J.H. Taylor	Mid-Surrey	St Andrews	309
1901	J. Braid	Romford	Muirfield	309
1902	A. Herd	Huddersfield	Hoylake	307
1903	H. Vardon	Totteridge	Prestwick	300
1904	J. White	Sunningdale	Sandwich	296
1905	J. Braid	Walton Heath	St Andrews	318
1906	J. Braid	Walton Heath	Muirfield	300
1907	A. Massy	La Boulie	Hoylake	312
1908	J. Braid	Walton Heath	Prestwick	291
1909	J.H. Taylor	Mid-Surrey	Deal	295
1910	J. Braid	Walton Heath	St Andrews	299
1911	H. Vardon	Totteridge	Sandwich	303
1912	E. Ray	Oxhey	Muirfield	295
1913	J.H. Taylor	Mid-Surrey	Hoylake	304
1914	H. Vardon	Totteridge	Prestwick	306
1915–19	No Championship			
1920	G. Duncan	Hanger Hill	Deal	303
1921	J. Hutchinson	USA	St Andrews	296
1922	W. Hagen	USA	Sandwich	300
1923	A.G. Havers	Coombe-Hill	Troon	295
1924	W. Hagen	USA	Hoylake	301
1925	J. Barnes	USA	Prestwick	300
1926	Mr R.T. Jones	USA	Royal Lytham & St Annes	291
1927	Mr R.T. Jones	USA	St Andrews	285
1928	W. Hagen	USA	Sandwich	292
1929	W. Hagen	USA	Muirfield	292
1930	Mr R.T. Jones	USA	Hoylake	291
1931	T.D. Armour	USA	Carnoustie	296
1932	G. Sarazen	USA	Prince's, Sandwich	283
1933	D. Shute	USA	St Andrews	292
1934	T.H. Cotton	Waterloo, Belgium	Sandwich	283
1935	A. Perry	Leatherhead	Muirfield	283

Year	Winner		Venue	Score
1936	A.H. Padgham	Sundridge Park	Hoylake	287
1937	T.H. Cotton	Ashridge	Carnoustie	290
1938	R.A. Whitcombe	Parkstone	Sandwich	295
1939	R. Burton	Sale	St Andrews	290
1940–45	No Championship			
1946	S. Snead	USA	St Andrews	290
1947	F. Daly	Balmoral	Hoylake	293
1948	T.H. Cotton	Royal Mid-Surrey	Muirfield	284
1949	A.D. Locke	SA	Sandwich	283
1950	A.D. Locke	SA	Troon	279
1951	M. Faulkner	Unattached	Royal Portrush	285
1952	A.D. Locke	SA	Royal Lytham	287
1953	B. Hogan	USA	Carnoustie	282
1954	P.W. Thomson	AUS	Royal Birkdale	283
1955	P.W. Thomson	AUS	St Andrews	281
1956	P.W. Thomson	AUS	Hoylake	286
1957	A.D. Locke	SA	St Andrews	279
1958	P.W. Thomson	AUS	Royal Lytham & St Annes	278
1959	G.J. Player	SA	Muirfield	284
1960	K.D.G. Nagle	AUS	St Andrews	278
1961	A.D. Palmer	USA	Royal Birkdale	284
1962	A.D. Palmer	USA	Troon	276
1963	R.J. Charles	NZ	Royal Lytham & St Annes	277
1964	A. Lema	USA	St Andrews	279
1965	P.W. Thomson	AUS	Royal Birkdale	285
1966	J.W. Nicklaus	USA	Muirfield	282
1967	R. de Vicenzo	ARG	Hoylake	278
1968	G.J. Player	SA	Carnoustie	289
1969	A. Jacklin	Potters Bar	Royal Lytham & St Annes	280
1970	J.W. Nicklaus	USA	St Andrews	283
1971	L. Trevino	USA	Royal Birkdale	278
1972	L. Trevino	USA	Muirfield	278
1973	T. Weiskopf	USA	Troon	276
1974	G.J. Player	SA	Royal Lytham & St Annes	282
1975	T. Watson	USA	Carnoustie	279
1976	J. Miller	USA	Royal Birkdale	279
1977	T. Watson	USA	Turnberry	268

Year	Winner	Venue	Score
1899	W. Smith	Baltimore	315
1900	H. Vardon, GB	Wheaton. Ill.	313
1901	L. Auchterlonie	Myopia. Mass.	315
1902	L. Auchterlonie, GB	Garden City	305
1903	W. Anderson	Baltusrol	307
1904	W. Anderson	Glenview	304
1905	W. Anderson	Myopia. Mass.	335
1906	A. Smith	Onwentsia	291
1907	A. Ross	Chestnut Hill, Pa.	302
1908	F. M'Leod	Myopia, Mass.	322
1909	G. Sargent	Englewood, N.J.	290
1910	A. Smith	Philadelphia	289
1911	J.J. M'Dermott	Wheaton. Ill.	307
1912	J.J. M'Dermott	Buffalo, N.Y.	294
1913	Mr F. Ouimet	Brookline. Mass.	304
1914	W. Hagen	Midlothian	297
1915	Mr J.D. Travers	Baltusrol	290
1916	Mr Charles Evans	Minneapolis	286
1919	W. Hagen	Braeburn	301
1920	E. Ray, GB	Inverness	295
1921	J. Barnes	Washington	289
1922	G. Sarazen	Glencoe	288
1923	Mr R.T. Jones	Inwood, L.I.	296
1924	C. Walker	Oakland Hills	297
1925	W. MacFarlane	Worcester	291
1926	Mr R.T. Jones	Scioto	293
1927	T.D. Armour	Oakmont	301
1928	J. Farrell	Olympia Fields	294
1929	Mr R.T. Jones	Winged Foot. New York	294
1930	Mr R.T. Jones	Interlachen	287
1931	B. Burke	Inverness	292
1932	G. Sarazen	Fresh Meadow	286
1933	Mr J. Goodman	North Shore	287
1934	O. Qutra	Merion	293
1935	S. Parks	Oakmont	299
1936	T. Manero	Springfield	282
1937	R. Guldahl	Oakland Hills	281
1938	R. Guldahl	Cherry Hills	284
1939	B. Nelson	Philadelphia	284
1940	W. Lawson Little	Canterbury, Ohio	287
1941	C. Wood	Fort Worth, Texas	284
1942–45	No Championship		
1946	L. Mangrum	Canterbury	284
1947	L. Worsham	St Louis	282
1948	B. Hogan	Los Angeles	276
1949	Dr C. Middlecoff	Medinah, Ill.	286
1950	B. Hogan	Merion, Pa.	287

AMERICAN OPEN CHAMPIONSHIP

Year	Winner	Venue	Score
1894	Willie Dunn, GB	New York, defeated Willie Campbell 2 holes	
1895	H.J. Rawlins	Newport	173
1896	J. Foulis	Southampton	152
1897	J. Lloyd	Wheaton. Ill.	162
1898	F. Herd	Shinnecock Hills	328

Year	Winner	Venue	Score
1951	B. Hogan	Oakland Hills, Mich.	287
1952	J. Boros	Dallas, Texas	281
1953	B. Hogan	Oakmont	283
1954	E. Furgol	Baltusrol	284
1955	J. Fleck	San Francisco	287
1956	Dr C. Middlecoff	Rochester	281
1957	R. Mayer	Inverness	282
1958	T. Bolt	Tulsa, Okla.	283
1959	W. Casper	Mamaroneck	282
1960	A.D. Palmer	Denver, Col.	280
1961	G. Littler	Birmingham, Mich.	281
1962	J.W. Nicklaus	Oakmont	283
1963	J. Boros	Brookline, Mass.	293
1964	K. Venturi	Washington	278
1965	G.J. Player, SA	St Louis, Miss.	282
1966	W. Casper	San Francisco	278
1967	J.W. Nicklaus	Baltusrol	275
1968	L. Trevino	Rochester	275
1969	O. Moody	Houston, Texas	281
1970	A. Jacklin, GB	Chaska, Minn.	281
1971	L. Trevino	Merion, Pa.	280
1972	J.W. Nicklaus	Pebble Beach	290
1973	J. Miller	Oakmont	279
1974	H. Irwin	Winged Foot, New York	287
1975	L. Graham	Medinah	287
1976	J. Pate	Atlanta	277
1977	H. Green	Southern Hills	278

AMERICAN PGA CHAMPIONSHIP

Year	Winner	Runner-up	Venue	Result
1916	J. Barnes	J. Hutchinson	Siwanoy	1 hole
1919	J. Barnes	F M'Leod	Engineers' Club	6 and 5
1920	W. Hutchinson	D. Edgar	Flossmoor	1 hole
1921	W. Hagen	E. French	Inwood Club	3 and 2
1922	G. Sarazen	E. French	Oakmont	4 and 3
1923	G. Sarazen	W. Hagen	Pelham	38th hole
1924	W. Hagen	J. Barnes	French Lick	2 holes
1925	W. Hagen	W.E. Mehlhorn	Olympia Fields	6 and 4
1926	W. Hagen	L. Diegel	Salisbury	4 and 3
1927	W. Hagen	J. Turnesa	Dallas, Texas	1 hole
1928	L. Diegel	A. Espinosa	Five Farms	6 and 5
1929	L. Diegel	J. Farrell	Hill Crest	6 and 4
1930	T.D. Armour	G. Sarazen	Fresh Meadow	1 hole
1931	T. Creavy	D. Shute	Wannamoisett	2 and 1
1932	O. Dutra	W. Walsh	St Paul, Minn.	4 and 3
1933	G. Sarazen	W. Goggin	Milwaukee	5 and 4
1934	P. Runyan	C. Wood	Buffalo	38th hole
1935	J. Revolta	T.D. Armour	Oklahoma	5 and 4
1936	D. Shute	J. Thomson	Pinehurst	3 and 2
1937	D. Shute	H. McSpaden	Pittsburgh	37th hole
1938	P. Runyan	S. Snead	Shawnee	8 and 7
1939	H. Picard	B. Nelson	Pomonok	37th hole
1940	B. Nelson	S. Snead	Hershey, Pa.	1 hole
1941	V. Ghezzie	B. Nelson	Denver, Colo.	38th hole
1942	S. Snead	J. Turnesa	Atlantic City	2 and 1
1943	No Championship			
1944	R. Hamilton	B. Nelson	Spokane, Wash.	1 hole
1945	B. Nelson	S. Byrd	Dayton, Ohio	4 and 3
1946	B. Hogan	E. Oliver	Portland	6 and 4
1947	J. Ferrier	C. Harbert	Detroit	2 and 1
1948	B. Hogan	M. Turnesa	Norwood Hills	7 and 6
1949	S. Snead	J. Palmer	Richmond, Va.	3 and 2
1950	C. Harper	H. Williams	Scioto, Ohio	4 and 3
1951	S. Snead	W. Burkemo	Oakmont, Pa.	7 and 6
1952	J. Turnesa	C. Harbert	Big Spring, Louisville	1 hole

AMERICAN MASTERS TOURNAMENT

Augusta National Golf Course, Augusta, Georgia

Year	Winner	Score
1934	H. Smith	284
1935	G. Sarazen	282
1936	H. Smith	285
1937	B. Nelson	283
1938	H. Picard	285
1939	R. Guldahl	279
1940	J. Demaret	280
1941	C. Wood	280
1942	B. Nelson	280
1943-45	No Championship	
1946	H. Keiser	282
1947	J. Demaret	281
1948	C. Harmon	279
1949	S. Snead	283
1950	J. Demaret	284
1951	B. Hogan	280
1952	S. Snead	286
1953	B. Hogan	274
1954	S. Snead	289
1955	C. Middlecoff	279
1956	J. Burke	289
1957	D. Ford	283
1958	A.D. Palmer	284
1959	A. Wall	284
1960	A.D. Palmer	282
1961	G.J. Player, SA	280
1962	A.D. Palmer	280
1963	J.W. Nicklaus	286
1964	A.D. Palmer	276
1965	J.W. Nicklaus	271
1966	J.W. Nicklaus	288
1967	G. Brewer	280
1968	R. Goalby	277
1969	G. Archer	281
1970	W. Casper	279
1971	C. Coody	279
1972	J.W. Nicklaus	286
1973	T. Aaron	283
1974	G.J. Player, SA	278
1975	J.W. Nicklaus	276
1976	R. Floyd	271
1977	T. Watson	276

Year	Winner	Runner-up	Venue	Result
1953	W. Burkemo	F. Lorza	Birmingham, Michigan	2 and 1
1954	C. Harbert	W. Burkemo	St Paul, Minn.	4 and 3
1955	D. Ford	C. Middlecoff	Detroit	4 and 3
1956	J. Burke	T. Kroll	Boston	3 and 2
1957	L. Hebert	D. Finsterwald	Miami Valley, Dayton	3 and 1
1958*	D. Finsterwald	W. Casper	Havertown, Penn.	276
1959	B. Rosburg	J. Barber	Minneapolis	277
1960	J. Hebert	J. Ferrier	Akron, Ohio	281
1961	J. Barber	D. January	Olympia Fields	277
1962	G.J. Player, SA	R. Goalby	Newtown Square	278
1963	J.W. Nicklaus	D. Ragan	Dallas, Texas	279
1964	R. Nichols	A.D. Palmer and J.W. Nicklaus	Columbus, Ohio	271
1965	D. Marr	W. Casper and J.W. Nicklaus	Ligonier, Penn.	280
1966	A. Geiberger	D. Wysong	Akron, Ohio	280
1967	D. January	A. Massengale	Denver, Col.	281
1968	J. Boros	A.D. Palmer and R.J. Charles	San Antonio	281
1969	R. Floyd	G.J. Player	Dayton, Ohio	276
1970	D. Stockton	A.D. Palmer and B. Murphy	Tulsa, Okla.	279
1971	J. Nicklaus	W. Casper	Palm Beach, Fla.	281
1972	G.J. Player, SA	T. Aaron and J. Jamieson	Birmingham, Mich.	281
1973	J.W. Nicklaus	B. Crampton	Canterbury, Cleveland	277
1974	L. Trevino	J. Nicklaus	Tanglewood, Winston Salem	276
1975	J.W. Nicklaus	B. Crampton	Firestone, Akron, Ohio	276
1976	D. Stockton	R. Floyd and D. January	Congressional	281
1977	L. Wadkins	G. Littler	Pebble Beach	

*From 1958, decided by stroke play.

Year	Winner	Runner-up	Venue	Result
1973	G.J. Player	G. Marsh	Wentworth	at 40th
1974	H. Irwin	G.J. Player	Wentworth	2 and 1
1975	H. Irwin	A. Geiberger	Wentworth	4 and 2
1976	D. Graham	H. Irwin	Wentworth	37th
1977	G. Marsh	R. Floyd	Wentworth	5 and 4

RYDER CUP

Year	Venue	Result
1927	Worcester Country Club, Worcester, Mass.	USA 9½ – 2½ Britain
1929	Moortown Golf Club, Leeds	Britain 7 – 5 USA
1931	Scioto Country Club, Columbus, Ohio	USA 9 – 3 Britain
1933	Southport & Ainsdale Golf Club, Southport	Britain 6½ – 5½ USA
1935	Ridgewood Country Club, Ridgewood. N.J.	USA 9 – 3 Britain
1937	Southport & Ainsdale Golf Club, Southport	USA 8 – 4 Britain
1947	Portland Golf Club, Portland, Oregon	USA 11 – 1 Britain
1949	Ganton Golf Club, Scarborough	USA 7 – 5 Britain
1951	Pinehurst Country Club, Pinehurst, N.C.	USA 9½ – 2½ Britain
1953	Wentworth Golf Club, Surrey	USA 6½ – 5½ Britain
1955	Thunderbird Country Club, Palm Springs	USA 8 – 4 Britain
1957	Lindrick Golf Club, Yorkshire	Britain 7½ – 4½ USA
1959	Eldorado Country Club, Palm Desert, Calif.	USA 8½ – 3½ Britain
1961	Royal Lytham & St Annes Golf Club, Lancs.	USA 14½ – 9½ Britain
1963	East Lake Country Club, Atlanta, Georgia	USA 23 – 9 Britain
1965	Royal Birkdale Golf Club, Southport	USA 19½ – 12½ Britain
1967	Champions Golf Club, Houston, Texas	USA 23½ – 8½ Britain
1969	Royal Birkdale Golf Club, Southport	USA 16 – 16 Britain
1971	Old Warson Country Club, St Louis	USA 18½ – 13½ Britain
1973	Muirfield, East Lothian	USA 19 – 13 Britain
1975	Laurel Valley, Ligonier, Penn.	USA 21 – 11 Britain
1977	Royal Lytham & St Annes Golf Club, Lancs.	USA 12½ – 7½ Britain

THE WORLD MATCH-PLAY CHAMPIONSHIP

Year	Winner	Runner-up	Venue	Result
1964	A.D. Palmer	N.C. Coles	Wentworth	2 and 1
1965	G.J. Player	P. Thomson	Wentworth	3 and 2
1966	G.J. Player	J.W. Nicklaus	Wentworth	6 and 4
1967	A.D. Palmer	P.W. Thomson	Wentworth	2 up
1968	G.J. Player	R.J. Charles	Wentworth	1 up
1969	R.J. Charles	G. Littler	Wentworth	at 37th
1970	J.W. Nicklaus	L. Trevino	Wentworth	2 and 1
1971	G.J. Player	J.W. Nicklaus	Wentworth	5 and 4
1972	T. Weiskopf	L. Trevino	Wentworth	4 and 3

THE BRITISH AMATEUR CHAMPIONSHIP

Year	Winner	Runner-up	Venue	Result
1885	A.F. MacFie	H.G. Hutchinson	Hoylake	7 and 6
1886	H.G. Hutchinson	H. Lamb	St Andrews	7 and 6
1887	H.G. Hutchinson	J. Ball	Hoylake	1 hole
1888	J. Ball	J.E. Laidlay	Prestwick	5 and 4
1889	J.E. Laidlay	L.M.B. Melville	St Andrews	2 and 1
1890	J. Ball	J.E. Laidlay	Hoylake	4 and 3
1891	J.E. Laidlay	H.H. Hilton	St Andrews	20th hole
1892	J. Ball	H.H. Hilton	Sandwich	3 and 1
1893	P. Anderson	J.E. Laidlay	Prestwick	1 hole

Year	Winner	Runner-up	Venue	Result
1894	John Ball	S.M. Fergusson	Hoylake	1 hole
1895	L.M.B. Melville	John Ball	St Andrews	19th hole
1896*	F.G. Tait	H.H. Hilton	Sandwich	8 and 7
1897	A.J.T. Allan	James Robb	Muirfield	4 and 2
1898	F.G. Tait	S.M. Fergusson	Hoylake	7 and 5
1899	J. Ball	F.G. Tait	Prestwick	37th hole
1900	H.H. Hilton	J. Robb	Sandwich	8 and 7
1901	H.H. Hilton	J.L. Low	St Andrews	1 hole
1902	C. Hutchings	S.H. Fry	Hoylake	1 hole
1903	R. Maxwell	H.G. Hutchinson	Muirfield	7 and 5
1904	W.J. Travis, USA	E. Blackwell	Sandwich	4 and 3
1905	A.G. Barry	Hon. O. Scott	Prestwick	3 and 2
1906	J. Robb	C.C. Lingen	Hoylake	4 and 3
1907	J. Ball	C.A. Palmer	St Andrews	6 and 4
1908	E.A. Lassen	H.E. Taylor	Sandwich	7 and 6
1909	R. Maxwell	Capt C.K. Hutchison	Muirfield	1 hole
1910	J. Ball	C. Aylmer	Hoylake	10 and 9
1911	H.H. Hilton	E.A. Lassen	Prestwick	4 and 3
1912	J. Ball	A. Mitchell	Westward Ho!	38th hole
1913	H.H. Hilton	R. Harris	St Andrews	6 and 5
1914	J.L.C. Jenkins	C.O. Hezlet	Sandwich	3 and 2
1915–19	No Championship			
1920	C.J.H. Tolley	R.A. Gardner, USA	Muirfield	37th hole
1921	W.I. Hunter	A.J. Graham	Hoylake	12 and 11
1922	E.W.E. Holderness	J. Caven	Prestwick	1 hole
1923	R.H. Wethered	R. Harris	Deal	7 and 6
1924	E.W.E. Holderness	E.F. Storey	St Andrews	3 and 2
1925	R. Harris	K.F. Fradgley	Westward Ho!	13 and 12
1926	J. Sweetser, USA	A.F. Simpson	Muirfield	6 and 5
1927	Dr W. Tweddell	D.E. Landale	Hoylake	7 and 6
1928	T.P. Perkins	R.H. Wethered	Prestwick	6 and 4
1929	C.J.H. Tolley	J.N. Smith	Sandwich	4 and 3
1930	R.T. Jones, USA	R.H. Wethered	St Andrews	7 and 6
1931	E. Martin Smith	J. De Forest	Westward Ho!	1 hole
1932	J. De Forest	E.W. Fiddian	Muirfield	3 and 1
1933	Hon. M. Scott	T.A. Bourn	Hoylake	4 and 3
1934	W. Lawson Little, USA	J. Wallace	Prestwick	14 and 13
1935	W. Lawson Little, USA	Dr W. Tweddell	Royal Lytham & St Annes	1 hole
1936	H. Thomson	J. Ferrier, AUS	St Andrews	2 holes
1937	R. Sweeny, Jun., USA	L.O. Munn	Sandwich	3 and 2
1938	C.R. Yates, USA	R.C. Ewing	Troon	3 and 2
1939	A.T. Kyle	A.A. Duncan	Hoylake	2 and 1
1940–45	No Championship			
1946	J. Bruen	R. Sweeny, USA	Birkdale	4 and 3

*Thirty-six holes played on and after this date.

Year	Winner	Runner-up	Venue	Result
1947	W.P. Turnesa, USA	R.D. Chapman, USA	Carnoustie	3 and 2
1948	F.R. Stranahan, USA	C. Stowe	Sandwich	5 and 4
1949	S.M. McCready	W.P. Turnesa, USA	Portmarnock	2 and 1
1950	F.R. Stranahan, USA	R.D. Chapman, USA	St Andrews	8 and 6
1951	R.D. Chapman, USA	C.R. Coe, USA	Porthcawl	5 and 4
1952	E. Harvie Ward, USA	F.R. Stranahan, USA	Prestwick	6 and 5
1953	J.B. Carr	E. Harvie Ward, USA	Hoylake	2 holes
1954	D.W. Bachli, AUS	W.C. Campbell, USA	Muirfield	2 and 1
1955	J.W. Conrad, USA	A. Slater	Royal Lytham & St Annes	3 and 2
1956†	J.C. Beharrell	L.G. Taylor	Troon	5 and 4
1957†	R. Reid Jack	H.B. Ridgley, USA	Formby	2 and 1
1958‡	J.B. Carr	A. Thirlwell	St Andrews	3 and 2
1959	D.R. Beman, USA	W. Hyndman, USA	Sandwich	3 and 2
1960	J.B. Carr	R. Cochran, USA	Portrush	8 and 7
1961	M.F. Bonallack	J. Walker	Turnberry	6 and 4
1962	R.D. Davies, USA	J. Povall	Hoylake	1 hole
1963	M.S.R. Lunt	J.G. Blackwell	St Andrews	2 and 1
1964	G.J. Clark	M.S.R. Lunt	Ganton	39th hole
1965	M.F. Bonallack	C.A. Clark	Porthcawl	2 and 1
1966	R.E. Cole, SA	R.D.B.M. Shade	Carnoustie (18 holes)	3 and 2
1967	R.B. Dickson, USA	R.J. Cerrudo, USA	Formby	2 and 1
1968	M.F. Bonallack	J B. Carr	Troon	7 and 6
1969	M.F. Bonallack	W. Hyndman, USA	Hoylake	3 and 2
1970	M.F. Bonallack	W. Hyndman, USA	Newcastle Co. Down	8 and 7
1971	S. Melnyk, USA	J. Simons, USA	Carnoustie	3 and 2
1972	T.W.B. Homer	A. Thirlwell	Royal St George's	4 and 3
1973	R. Siderowf, USA	P.H. Moody	Royal Porthcawl	5 and 3
1974	T.W.B. Homer	J. Gabrielson	Muirfield	2 holes
1975	V. Giles	M. James	Hoylake	8 and 7
1976	R. Siderowf, USA	J. Davies	St Andrews	37th hole
1977	P. McEvoy	H. Campbell	Ganton	5 and 4

†In 1956 and 1957 the Quarter Finals, Semi Finals and Final were played over 36 holes.

‡In 1958 Semi Finals and Final only were played over 36 holes.

Index

COURSES

TOURNAMENTS